Traditional Holiday Fare

Recipes from Canada's East Coast

with **Saltscapes** *Food Editor*

Marie Nightingale

PLUS festive decorating ideas

SALTSCAPES
canada's east coast magazine

NIMBUS PUBLISHING

Nimbus Publishing Limited
PO Box 9166, Halifax, NS   B3K 5M8
(902) 455-4286

Saltscapes Publishing Limited
40 Alderney Drive, Suite 501, Dartmouth, NS   B2Y 2N5
(902) 464-7258

Printed and bound in Canada

Photo Credits

All photography by Perry Jackson, with the exception of:
Cork photo, page 23: Wonderfile
Turkey photo, page 38: BMP Stock Photo
Wreath photos, pages 44-45: Kevin Yarr

Library and Archives Canada Cataloguing in Publication

    Traditional holiday fare : recipes from Canada's east coast / with Saltscapes food editor, Marie Nightingale.
    Includes index.
    Co-published by Saltscapes.
    ISBN 1-55109-512-2

1. Christmas cookery—Atlantic Provinces. I. Nightingale, Marie II. Title: Saltscapes.

TX739.T73 2004   641.5'68   C2004-905149-0

Canadä   The Canada Council | Le Conseil des Arts
          for the Arts | du Canada

We acknowledge the financial support of the Government of Canada through the Book Publishing Industry Development Program (BPIDP) and the Canada Council for our publishing activities.

Acknowledgements

Since holidays, however they are celebrated, are family affairs, I would be remiss if I didn't acknowledge my sons, Frank, Gary and Bob, my daughters-in-law, Sarah and Pamela, and my grandchildren, Craig and Ashley, Candice, Christa and Corey. All play a role in making the memories I treasure.

Further back were the wonderful Christmases spent with Laurie's parents, his sisters and their families, when the dining room table at Oakland Road easily stretched to accommodate 20 or more. Earlier still were holidays celebrated with my own siblings, when although threatened, none of us ever found a piece of coal in our Christmas stocking. A 64-page book can't begin to hold the many special memories.

And now, there is another "family" helping to make memories. These are my friends and colleagues at Saltscapes. Headed by Jim and Linda Gourlay, who accepted the collaboration with Nimbus Publishing to put out this book of traditional holiday fare, they very wisely placed it in the talented and capable hands of production manager Shawn Dalton and editor Line Goguen-Hughes.

Throughout the book Perry Jackson's photography brings a festive touch to the food, some of which was prepared for photographing by Chef Brian Lange, while more was arranged by food stylist Sarah Werth. And Bass River Chairs in the Halifax Shopping Centre was always happy to provide tableware and linens.

I am grateful to have had the opportunity of working again with Sandra McIntyre, Helen Matheson and Heather Bryan, of Nimbus, along with Dan Soucoup, who will hopefully sell a million copies!

Also to be thanked are the friends and readers whose recipes grace the pages and provide delicious eating throughout the chapters.

I thank you all. And my best wish for each of you is that you will enjoy a wonderful holiday season, however you celebrate it.

contents

Traditional Holiday Fare

Saltscapes is just a baby where magazines are concerned. But we're growing and gaining new readers every year. During our five years of publication, we have published only four holiday issues, but that was enough to warrant attention from you, our dear readers, and from Nimbus Publishing, who suggested we do a holiday cookbook.

So, we're dishing up a second helping. Not only are there holiday recipes from the pages of Saltscapes, but also from my cookbooks—mainly *Marie Nightingale's Favourite Recipes*, published in 1993 and now out of print. Interspersed are recipes I just couldn't resist including.

Those of you who know me, know my style, which includes wishing you the happiest of holidays. May your memories of earlier celebrations be repeated again and again, with perhaps a new trend or two added for excitement.

✳

The holiday season in the Atlantic Provinces has always meant family, food, festivities and fudge. You can add fruitcake as well, dark, light or both.

For me, the build-up to Christmas was even better than opening the presents. It started with rehearsals for the school concert when children donned crepe paper costumes and moved to a higher level as angels, or remained earthbound as shepherds carrying crooked sticks for staffs. I never got to be an angel, but one year I was the baby doll in the March of the Wooden Soldiers. In a long nightgown and baby bonnet, with hands outstretched and moving up and down in time with the martial music, I led the other "toys" onto the

stage and felt quite important in my non-speaking role.

Anticipation accelerated as each day after school I would be met with wonderful aromas wafting from the kitchen as once-a-year treats were baked and hoarded into cupboards.

Part of the excitement lay in decorating the house. Children would occupy themselves for hours as they pasted strips of tissue paper into chains, alternating the red and the green "links." Twisted strands of crepe paper were also part of the decoration, running from each corner of the ceiling to the centre light fixture. Sometimes tinsel would be hung over the strands, as well as on the spruce boughs adorning every painting or picture on the walls. Strings of popcorn and cranberries were also made by little hands, in preparation for the night that Santa would wrap them around the tree standing bare in the corner. The question of how he managed to do this in every home never crossed the children's minds, perhaps for fear that knowing would make the magic disappear. In faith they left out milk and cookies before reluctantly making their way to bed.

But the wonderment of it all, when children lined up to come down the stairs together and catch the first glimpse of the sparkling lights and gingerbread ornaments! Each year, the tree was more beautiful than the one before, even though it was always the same.

And then the stockings, with the crayons and colouring books, paper dolls and trinkets…just before you got to the precious orange in the toe, there was a red or yellow clear toy candy in the shape of a train, a turkey, a Santa, a boot, a horse,

or any number of animal shapes. This was the treat of the season, made by Robertson's Candy, a small but sweet company still operating in Truro today.

In the home that I shared with my husband Laurie and our three sons, Frank, Gary and Bobby (who now prefers to be called Bob), long-held traditions carried through. Certainly, there were adaptations as we merged our childhood customs to the satisfaction of both. I managed to live without the potato dressing that stuffed the turkey of my youth, while Laurie seemed to willingly accept the "new" foods that would be quietly incorporated. Everything, that is, except dates!

As for the gifts, well, they were of the kind that I couldn't even have imagined as a girl growing up in the Depression years.

Today, another generation follows the holiday customs of their youth. There will be a touch of impatience (disguised perhaps, but nevertheless, it exists) as the current head of the household struggles to get the camera operating. And on the dining table the traditional breakfast of orange "smiles" and oatmeal porridge remains intact, although the additional choice of a Mimosa is offered, along with plain orange juice.

These are among my memories of Christmases past, both early and later.

❋

But in other homes, different traditions prevail, set by people of the various ethnic backgrounds that form the cultural tapestry of Atlantic Canada.

Those of English descent continue to stir up their plum puddings. The Irish have

their porter cake, and the Scots their black bun and Hogmanay shortbread. The Germans prefer carrot pudding and prepare a hot kohl slaw to accompany the roast turkey, while the Lebanese prefer their turkey stuffed with lamb, followed by a dessert of layered pastry, called Baglawa. A Christmas Eve tradition among the Portuguese is a dinner of salted codfish, potatoes and cabbage, while the Ukranians celebrate with borsch and holubsti (rice-filled cabbage). Scandinavians often begin their smorgasbord with glogg or acquavit (water of life), and end it with julekage (fruit loaf); the Dutch must have their marzipan and peppernuts, while the Greeks enjoy their turkey with chestnut stuffing, and honey cakes for dessert. In the past, the Polish Wigila meal usually consisted of 12 courses, but today a fruit compote might be served, followed by an array of fish, salads, marinated herring, sauerkraut and a variety of desserts. And, in Jewish homes, fried foods such as latkes (potato pancakes) and fried Hanukkah cookies are served as part of the eight-day Hanukkah celebrations.

Each culture woven into the Down East tapestry—with its own religious and cultural observances, whether it be Christmas, Hanukkah, Ramadan or Divali, among others—carries its own traditions, which have been honoured and celebrated through the centuries.

Enjoy yours.

holiday baking

Here in the Atlantic Provinces, holiday preparations often begin with the making of green tomato mincemeat for the pies and tarts that will follow. By October, in many homes, raisins are being put to soak in an alcoholic bath to ready them for the traditional fruitcake and plum pudding, baked at least a month in advance of the celebration.

In Victorian times, preparations for the fruitcake and pudding would start on Stir-up Sunday, the last Sunday before Advent begins. It was important that each member of the family take a hand in the stirring, a promise of good luck. In many homes the tradition still holds, but with modifications. Fruitcakes have been lightened or replaced with cherry cakes, while carrot and cranberry puddings have become almost as popular as the old English "plum."

Once the cakes are made and wrapped for aging, pie baking begins. Tradition still calls for mince pies, although the meat of earlier recipes is usually omitted, being replaced by apples, raisins, and yes, green tomatoes. Apple pies can also be made ahead and stored in the freezer, along with quick breads and mince tarts.

And now, the real baking begins. No food —not mincemeat pie, pudding, or even fruitcake—can make up for a shortage of cookies at this special time of year. Old spices are thrown out and replaced by fresh supplies of cinnamon, ginger, cloves and nutmeg. Molasses, butter, nuts and coconut are also on the shopping list, while supplies of flour and sugar, both white and brown, are checked.

Every family has its own favourite recipes, passed down through the generations and served year after year, and if the selection is varied enough, it will be hard to improve on a tray full of cookies set out with mugs of hot mulled cider or hot chocolate.

George-Anne's Cake

When George-Anne Merrill of Halifax was in the catering business a few years back, her fruitcake was always on the menu for holiday parties and events. Even people who claimed they didn't like fruitcake changed their tune when they sampled this whiskey-soaked "cake with a kick."

In a large bowl, combine raisins, cherries, and bourbon; cover and refrigerate overnight. Drain well, reserving bourbon. Grease well a 10-inch (25 cm) deep round cake pan or spring-form pan, line with wax paper, grease again, and dust with flour. Also, prepare a 9x5-inch (23x13 cm) loaf pan in the same way. Set both aside. (A 10-inch/25-cm tube pan and two small loaf pans may be used instead, or use several small loaf pans to make small cakes to give as gifts.) Preheat oven to 275°F (140°C). Place a small metal bowl with water on the bottom shelf of the oven. (This helps to keep the cake moist.)

In large mixer bowl, cream butter until fluffy. Gradually add the sugars, mixing until light and well blended. Beat in egg yolks.

Set aside 1/2 cup (125 mL) of the flour to dust pecans. In a separate bowl or on a sheet of wax paper, sift together remaining 4 1/2 cups (1.125 L) of flour, baking powder, salt and nutmeg. Add to creamed mixture alternately with bourbon, making three additions of flour and two of bourbon.

Beat egg whites until stiff but not dry; fold into batter. Dust pecans with reserved flour; fold into batter. Fold in raisins and cherries. Pour batter into prepared 10-inch (25 cm) pan to within 1 inch (2.5 cm) of top. Pour remaining batter into loaf pan. Bake large cake for 4 1/2 hours, and loaf cake for 2 1/2 hours. Start testing large cake for doneness after 3 1/2 hours, smaller cake after 2 hours. The cakes are done when a toothpick inserted in centre comes out dry, and cakes feels firm when lightly pressed with a finger.

Remove from oven; cool 15 minutes. Peel off paper, and place cakes on racks to cool completely. Wrap cakes in cheesecloth, brush with bourbon, rewrap in plastic wrap and foil. Seal tightly and put in a cool dry place to age. Each week, carefully unwrap the cakes, brush with more bourbon and reseal. Cakes should age for at least 3 weeks before serving.

ingredients

2 cups (500 mL) white seedless raisins

2 cups (500 mL) red candied cherries

2 cups (500 mL) bourbon

2 cups (500 mL) butter

2 cups (500 mL) granulated sugar

2 cups (500 mL) dark brown sugar

8 eggs, separated

5 cups (1.25 L) all-purpose flour

1 1/2 teaspoons (7 mL) baking powder

1 teaspoon (5 mL) salt

2 teaspoons (10 mL) freshly grated nutmeg

4 cups (1 L) pecan halves

Anna's Gumdrop Cake

This holiday cake, said to have originated in the Maritimes during the early 1930s, is still a favourite holiday treat throughout Atlantic Canada. Be sure to leave out any black gumdrops, or you won't like the colour they impart.

Cut gumdrops into small pieces with wet scissors; dredge with about 1/3 cup (75 mL) of the flour. Grease a deep 8x8x3-inch (20x20x8 cm) cake pan and line with heavy brown paper. Grease again. Set aside.

In a large bowl, thoroughly cream butter. Gradually add sugar, beating well after each addition. Add eggs, one at a time, beating well after each addition.

Combine remaining flour with baking powder and salt. Blend into creamed mixture alternately with milk, beginning and ending with dry ingredients. Stir in vanilla, lemon extract and gumdrops.

Turn batter into prepared pan and bake at 350°F (180°C) for 1 to 1 1/2 hours or until cake tester inserted in centre comes out clean. Let cool in pan on a wire rack for 10 to 15 minutes before turning out for complete cooling.

ingredients

- 1 pound (500 g) gumdrops (omit black ones)
- 3 cups (750 mL) all-purpose flour
- 1 cup (250 mL) butter (or 1/2 cup (125 mL) butter and 1/2 cup (125 mL) margarine, softened
- 2 cups (500 mL) granulated sugar
- 3 eggs
- 1 teaspoon (5 mL) baking powder
- 1/2 teaspoon (2 mL) salt
- 1 cup (250 mL) milk
- 1/2 teaspoon (2 mL) vanilla
- 1/2 teaspoon (2 mL) lemon extract

Chocolate Pound Cake

To some, Christmas comes by the pound. Pound cake, which once incorporated a pound each of butter, sugar, eggs and flour, has been lightened and flavoured in various ways to satisfy today's discriminating tastes. One of the current favourites is chocolate.

Grease a 10-inch (25 cm) tube or Bundt pan and dust with sifted cocoa powder. Sift together the flour, baking powder and salt.

In large mixer bowl, cream butter until smooth. Gradually add sugar, beating until the mixture is light and fluffy. Add vanilla. Add eggs, one at a time, beating well after each addition. Add sifted cocoa powder. Add dry ingredients alternately with milk (4 additions of flour and 3 of milk), beating well after each addition.

Pour into prepared pan and bake at 325°F (160°C) for 1 hour and 20 minutes or until a cake tester inserted in centre comes out clean. Invert onto a wire rack until cool. Dust with sifted icing sugar, if desired.

ingredients

- 3 cups (750 mL) sifted all-purpose flour
- 1 tablespoon (15 mL) baking powder
- 1/4 teaspoon (1 mL) salt
- 1 cup (250 mL) butter, softened
- 3 cups (750 mL) sugar
- 1 tablespoon (15 mL) vanilla
- 3 eggs
- 1 cup (250 mL) unsweetened cocoa powder, sifted
- 1 1/2 cups (375 mL) milk
- Icing sugar, optional

Christmas Plum Pudding

Debbe Bridges Hinchey has fond memories of the Christmas pudding her mother made in O'Leary, PEI. The delicious sauce was Debbe's great-grandmother's.

Pick raisins apart and place in a large bowl. Drain cherries and pat dry; add to raisins. Toss fruit with 1/2 cup (125 mL) of the flour. Sift remaining flour with salt, baking soda and spices. Grease well three 48-ounce (1.36 L) juice cans (smaller cans may be used).

In mixer, cream butter until smooth. Add molasses, eggs and vanilla; mix well. Stir in buttermilk. Gradually add dry ingredients; mix until combined. Add fruit; mix well. Spoon batter into cans, filling two-thirds full. Cover tops with a double layer of foil, leaving a 2-inch (5 cm) overhang; tie securely with string.

Place filled cans on a rack in a large pot. Add enough boiling water to come half-way up cans. Cover pot, bring to a boil, reduce heat to maintain a moderate boil. Steam for 2 to 3 hours, adding more boiling water if necessary. After 2 hours, insert a toothpick into centre of pudding; if it comes out clean, the pudding is done. (Small puddings need less time.)

Remove puddings from pot, place on a rack to cool for 15 minutes. Turn out to cool completely. Wrap tightly in plastic wrap or foil and store in refrigerator for up to 2 weeks. Freeze for longer storage. To serve, steam in original can for 45 minutes. Serve with sauce.

ingredients

- 2 pounds (1 kg) seeded (Lexia) raisins
- 1 small container (225 g) glacé red cherries, halved
- 1 small container (225 g) glacé green cherries, halved
- 1 large container (450 g) chopped mixed glacé fruit
- 3 cups (750 mL) flour (or more, if needed)
- 1/2 teaspoon (2 mL) salt
- 1 1/2 teaspoons (7 mL) baking soda
- 1 1/2 teaspoons (7 mL) ground allspice
- 1/2 teaspoon (2 mL) grated nutmeg
- 1 cup (250 mL) butter, softened
- 1 1/2 cups (375 mL) molasses
- 2 large eggs, beaten
- 1 teaspoon (5 mL) vanilla
- 1 1/2 cups (375 mL) buttermilk

Brown Sugar Sauce

Melt butter in a saucepan over medium-low heat. Add brown sugar, stirring constantly until sugar liquifies and becomes amber in colour, being careful not to let it burn. This caramelization gives the sauce its wonderful flavour. Stir in salt and flour and cook 2 to 3 minutes. Gradually add water, stirring constantly as it comes to a boil. Cook for 5 minutes. Add flavouring. Serve hot over plum pudding.

ingredients

- 1/4 cup (50 mL) butter
- 1 cup (250 mL) packed dark brown sugar
- 1/2 teaspoon (2 mL) salt
- 4 tablespoons (60 mL) flour
- 2 cups (500 mL) boiling water
- 2 tablespoons (30 mL) brandy or 1 tablespoon (15 mL) vanilla

Marianne's Honey Cake

A typical Hanukkah meal at the home of Marianne Ferguson, in Halifax, might include chicken soup with noodles, roast chicken, potato latkes with applesauce, a green salad with oil and vinegar dressing, Hanukkah cookies, and Marianne's award-winning honey cake.

ingredients

1 orange

4 eggs

1 cup (250 mL) granulated sugar

1/2 cup (125 mL) vegetable oil

1 cup (250 mL) liquid honey

2 1/2 cups (625 mL) all-purpose flour

3 teaspoons (15 mL) baking powder

1/2 teaspoon (2 mL) baking soda

1/2 teaspoon (2 mL) salt

1/2 teaspoon (2 mL) ground cloves

1/2 cup (125 mL) strong cold tea or coffee

Ginger, allspice, raisins, nuts, to taste

If using a food processor, chop whole, seeded orange; if using a mixer, use only grated rind and juice. Add eggs, sugar, oil and honey; beat until light and creamy.

Combine flour, baking powder, soda, salt and cloves; add to first mixture. (Spices such as ginger or allspice may be added, as well as raisins and nuts, according to your tastes.) Pour in tea and mix well.

Pour batter into a greased 10-inch (25 cm) Bundt pan and bake at 350°F (180°C) for 1 to 1 1/2 hours. (If cake appears to be browning too quickly, either reduce the heat to 325°F [160°C] or lay a piece of foil over top of pan.) Cake is done when a cake tester inserted in centre comes out completely clean.

Cool in pan on a wire rack for 1 hour. Turn out on wire rack and cool completely.

Nut-crusted Truffle Pie

*We had a lot of positive feedback when we ran this recipe in **Saltscapes** in 2003. It's well worth making again, especially since it can be prepared ahead and refrigerated.*

Crust: In a bowl, mix together ground and chopped nuts. Add sugar and melted butter; stir to mix well. Press mixture into bottom and up sides of a 10-inch (25 cm) glass pie plate. Bake in a 350°F (180°C) oven until lightly browned, about 15 minutes. Set on a rack to cool.

Filling: In the top of a double boiler, over hot—not boiling—water, melt chocolate. Add butter and, when melted, stir to blend thoroughly with chocolate. Remove from heat. Stir in egg yolks, vanilla and instant coffee. Add brandy, stirring until blended. Fold in whipped cream and stiffly beaten egg whites. Pour filling into nut crust and refrigerate overnight or at least 8 hours before serving. Makes 8 servings.

crust:

1 cup (250 mL) freshly ground walnuts

3/4 cup (175 mL) freshly ground pecans

1/2 cup (125 mL) finely chopped pecans

1/3 cup (75 mL) granulated sugar

3 tablespoons (45 mL) butter, melted and cooled

filling:

8 ounces (225 g) bittersweet chocolate

1/4 cup (50 mL) butter

4 eggs, separated

1 teaspoon (5 mL) vanilla

1/4 teaspoon (1 mL) instant coffee

2 tablespoons (30 mL) brandy

1 cup (250 mL) whipping cream, whipped stiff

Mistletoe Pie in Chocolate Coconut Crust

Ice cream and sherbet are popular any time of the year, but they're even more special when served in a chocolate coconut crust and topped with a raspberry sauce.

Prepare crust: In top of a double boiler over hot—not boiling—water, melt chocolate and butter, stirring until blended.

In a small bowl, combine milk and icing sugar; add to chocolate mixture, stirring well. Add coconut and stir well. Spread on bottom and up sides of a greased 9-inch (23 cm) pie plate. Chill until firm.

Filling: Spoon softened ice cream into crust, spreading evenly over bottom and up the sides. Place in freezer until firm. Spoon softened sherbet over ice cream, spreading evenly and packing lightly so it adheres to ice cream layer. Wrap pie in foil and place in freezer until firm.

When ready to serve, place thawed raspberries with their juice in a saucepan. In a cup, combine sugar and cornstarch; stir into berries and cook over low heat, stirring all the while, until thickened. Spoon sauce over pie wedges while warm and serve. Makes 8 servings.

crust:

2 ounces (2 squares) unsweetened chocolate

2 tablespoons (30 mL) butter

2 tablespoons (30 mL) hot milk or water

2/3 cup (150 mL) sifted icing sugar

1 1/2 cups (375 mL) flaked or desiccated coconut, toasted or plain

filling:

2 cups (500 mL) vanilla ice cream, softened

2 cups (500 mL) lime sherbet, softened

2 cups (500 mL) frozen raspberries, thawed, not drained

1 tablespoon (15 mL) sugar

1 1/2 tablespoons (22 mL) cornstarch

Apple-Cranberry-Mince Pie

If regular mincemeat is too heavy for you, this recipe may be made to order. Because it calls for only a small amount, it's a handy recipe for using up mincemeat left over from other baking. It's an apple, cranberry and mince pie all rolled up in one. It's one of my favourite pies.

Divide dough in half; roll out one half and fit into a 9-inch (23 cm) pie plate, leaving a 3/4-inch (2 cm) overhang.

In a large bowl, combine apples, cranberries and mincemeat.

In a separate bowl, combine sugar and flour. Sprinkle 1/4 cup (50 mL) of the sugar mixture over bottom of pastry-lined pie plate. Add fruit mixture and spread evenly. Combine orange juice and salt and sprinkle over fruit. Spoon remaining sugar mixture over fruit.

Roll out remaining dough. Using a pastry-cutting wheel and a ruler to guide it, cut into 10 strips about 1/2 inch (1 cm) wide, and keeping the strips about an inch (2.5 cm) apart, form a lattice top. Trim ends of strips even with crust overhang. Press together, fold edge under and flute.

Bake in a preheated 400°F (200°C) oven for 10 minutes. Reduce heat to 350°F (180°C) and bake 30 to 40 minutes longer, or until crust is golden and filling is bubbling. Makes 6 to 8 servings.

ingredients

Pastry for a double crust 9-inch (23 cm) pie

4 cups (1 L) thinly sliced apples, pared and cored

1 cup (250 mL) fresh cranberries, cut in half

1/4 cup (50 mL) mincemeat

1 1/4 cups (300 mL) sugar

3 tablespoons (45 mL) all-purpose flour

2 tablespoons (30 mL) orange juice

1/2 teaspoon (2 mL) salt

Green Tomato Mincemeat Pie

The recipe for Green Tomato Mincemeat is found on page 55, and if you are fortunate enough to have put a supply down at the end of the harvest, here is how to make the pie.

Divide dough into 2 equal portions. Roll one portion and line a 9-inch (23 cm) pie plate. Roll second portion, fold, and cut vents.

Combine mincemeat, apples, and liquor, if using. Ladle into lined pie plate. Cover with vented top crust. Bake at 425°F (220°C) for 15 minutes; reduce heat to 350°F (180°C) and bake 30 minutes longer, or until golden brown.

ingredients

Pastry for 1 double crust 9-inch (23 cm) pie

3 cups (750 mL) green tomato mincemeat (see page 55)

1 cup (250 mL) chopped apple

1/4 cup (50 mL) rum or brandy (optional)

ingredients

Pastry for a single 9-inch (23 cm) pie

1 cup (250 mL) dates, cut up

Water

1/2 cup (125 mL) packed brown sugar

2 eggs, separated

1 tablespoon (15 mL) butter or margarine

1 teaspoon (5 mL) vanilla

2 cups (500 mL) evaporated milk

1/2 teaspoon (2 mL) salt

meringue

3 egg whites

1/4 (1 mL) teaspoon cream of tartar

6 tablespoons (90 mL) granulated or
   superfine sugar

Date Meringue Pie

Although dates have lost some of the popularity they once enjoyed, this old-fashioned pie could be instrumental in bringing them back—with honours.

Roll dough into a circle and trim 1 inch (2.5 cm) larger than an upside-down pie plate. Press dough into pie plate, fold edge under and flute.

In saucepan, combine dates with just enough water to cover. Cook 5 minutes or until soft, stirring frequently. Stir in brown sugar. Remove from heat.

In small bowl, beat egg yolks slightly (reserve whites for meringue). Add to date mixture, along with butter, vanilla, milk and salt. Mix well and pour into unbaked pie shell. Bake at 350°F (180°C) for 30 minutes or until filling bubbles up well and knife inserted in centre comes out clean.

Remove from oven and cover with plastic wrap to keep hot and prevent skin from forming.

To make meringue for a 9-inch (23 cm) pie: Have bowl and beaters well chilled. Have egg whites at room temperature.

In bowl, combine egg whites with cream of tartar and beat until foamy. Gradually beat in sugar one tablespoon (15 mL) at a time. Continue beating 1 1/2 to 2 minutes or until mixture is glossy and stiff peaks form.

Carefully remove plastic wrap from pie while still warm and spread meringue over filling. Push some of the meringue securely against crust to seal and to prevent it from shrinking. Pile meringue lightly and quickly, swirling and lifting to form attractive peaks (do not overwork). Bake at 350°F (180°C) for 15 minutes or until meringue is golden. Cool on rack at room temperature away from drafts. Treat as a cream pie and store in refrigerator if not using within 2 hours. Makes 6 or 8 servings.

Snickerdoodles

While my boys were growing up, cookie-making took precedence over all other types of baking, especially during the weeks leading up to Christmas. Once baked and cooled, the cookies would be packed into tins and stored in the freezer. So ambitious was I in providing variety, that one year the supply lasted until Easter. Snickerdoodles were a family favourite.

In large mixer bowl, thoroughly cream butter or margarine. Gradually add sugar and cream well. Add eggs and beat well.

In a separate bowl, sift together flour, cream of tartar, baking soda and salt. Add to creamed mixture and stir until blended. Turn dough out onto large piece of wax paper. Wrap, and put in refrigerator to chill for about an hour.

In small dish, combine topping ingredients.

Remove dough from fridge and roll into 1-inch (2.5 cm) balls. Roll balls in cinnamon-sugar mixture. Place on ungreased cookie sheets 2 inches (5 cm) apart. Bake at 400°F (200°C) for 8 to 10 minutes, until lightly browned but still soft. Cookies will puff up at first, then flatten out with crinkled tops. Makes about 5 dozen cookies.

ingredients

1 cup (250 mL) butter or margarine

1 1/2 cups (375 mL) granulated sugar

2 eggs

2 3/4 cups (675 mL) all-purpose flour

2 teaspoons (10 mL) cream of tartar

1 teaspoon (5 mL) baking soda

1/2 teaspoon (2 mL) salt

topping

2 tablespoons (30 mL) sugar

1 teaspoon (5 mL) cinnamon

"Scratch-Me-Back" Cookies

"My mother, Erminie Anderson, of Lockeport, Shelburne County, has passed down this recipe to me. It also appears in my Aunt Alexia's old recipe book and is credited to Mrs. 'Hen Bill' (Mrs. Henry Bill). The Bill family goes back several generations in Lockeport." – Helen Hall, Butter the Size of an Egg *(The Yarmouth County Historical Society)*

This traditional cookie is based on the ever-popular combination of rolled oats and coconut. Whoever came up with the eye-catching name must have had a good sense of humour.

ingredients

1 cup (250 mL) shortening (or 1/2 cup/125 mL butter and 1/2 cup/125 mL shortening)

1 cup (250 mL) brown sugar

1 egg

1 teaspoon (5 mL) vanilla

1 cup (250 mL) rolled oats

1 cup (250 mL) flour

1 1/2 (375 mL) cups coconut

1/2 (2 mL) teaspoon baking soda

1/2 (2 mL) teaspoon baking powder

Cream shortening, sugar, egg and vanilla. Add all ingredients and mix well. Roll into small balls and place on cookie sheet. Flatten well with fork. Bake in a 350°F (180°C) oven about 8 minutes.

Maizie's Loyalist Molasses Cookies

Bill Crowell tells this story in Butter the Size of an Egg, *a cookbook presented by the Yarmouth County Historical Society: "When I was living in Lockeport as a boy, I regularly asked my mother to make big, fat molasses cookies like Mrs. Swansburg always made. She would say yes, but what we always got were ginger snaps—my father's favourite.*

"Years later, my wife Fran and I moved to the South Shore, to teach at Shelburne Regional High School. One day, walking downtown, I spotted a half-eaten molasses cookie at the edge of the sidewalk in front of Cox's store. I enthused to Fran. Little Christine, who was two or three years old, wanted to eat it!

"At school, in the staff room, Fran announced the problem. 'We can't find such a recipe.' Maizie Bruce said, 'My mother made them and I'll look through her recipe book.' The very next day Maizie showed up with this recipe. Maizie believes it came to Shelburne with the Loyalists."

ingredients
1 cup (250 mL) sugar
1 cup (250 mL) shortening
1 cup (250 mL) molasses
3 eggs, beaten
1 tablespoon (15 mL) vinegar
4 cups (1 L) flour
2 teaspoons (10 mL) baking soda, scant
1 teaspoon (5 mL) salt
1 teaspoon (5 mL) cinnamon
2 teaspoons (10 mL) ginger
white sugar and raisins for decoration

Cream sugar and shortening. Add molasses, eggs and vinegar. Blend well. Add sifted dry ingredients. Roll out and cut some with circular cutter, and the others should be ginger bread men. Sprinkle with sugar, add raisin eyes, mouth and buttons. Bake at 350°F (180°C) for 12 to 15 minutes.

Gumdrop Cookies

Here is another old-fashioned cookie that has passed the test of time in Atlantic Canada. The popular combination of oatmeal and coconut is enhanced by cut-up gumdrops, to add flavour and colour. Black gumdrops should not be used.

ingredients

1 cup (250 mL) shortening, softened

1 cup (250 mL) packed brown sugar

1 cup (250 mL) granulated sugar

2 eggs

1 teaspoon (5 mL) vanilla

2 cups (500 mL) all-purpose flour

1 teaspoon (5 mL) baking powder

1/2 teaspoon (2 mL) baking soda

1/2 teaspoon (2 mL) salt

2 cups (500 mL) quick rolled oats

1 cup (250 mL) coconut

1 cup (250 mL) baking gumdrops, halved (no black)

Cream shortening and sugars until light and fluffy. Add eggs and beat well. Add vanilla.

Combine flour, baking powder, soda and salt and add to creamed mixture. Stir in rolled oats, coconut and gumdrops. Shape into 1-inch (2.5 cm) balls, place on a lightly greased foil-lined cookie sheet and flatten with a fork. Bake at 350°F (180°C) for 10 minutes, or until lightly browned and set. Makes 6 dozen cookies.

Sheila's Cocoa Shortbread Cookies

I once made these cookies on a very hot day, when the butter turned almost to oil. Chilling didn't do the trick, so I simply shaped the dough into 1-inch (2.5 cm) balls and pressed them down with a fork. They were just as tasty and saved the rolling procedure. The dough can also be shaped into two 1 1/2-inch (4 cm) rolls and chilled, then sliced to the same thickness and baked.

Sift together flour, cocoa powder and salt; stir well and set aside. In large mixer bowl, cream butter until light and fluffy.

Gradually add icing sugar, beating until smooth. Add vanilla. Gradually add flour mixture, stirring well to combine. Chill for at least 1 hour.

Divide dough into three portions and roll out on a lightly floured surface to a little less than 1/4 inch (5 mm) thickness. Cut out shapes with a floured cookie cutter. Place on ungreased foil-lined baking sheets. Bake at 350°F (180°C) for 10 to 12 minutes. Makes about 3 dozen cookies.

ingredients

2 cups (500 mL) all-purpose flour

1/3 cup (75 mL) sifted cocoa powder

1/2 teaspoon (2 mL) salt

1 1/4 cups (300 mL) butter, softened

1 1/3 cups (325 mL) sifted icing sugar

1 1/2 teaspoons (7 mL) vanilla

ingredients

2 1/2 cups (625 mL) all-purpose flour

2 tablespoons (30 mL) granulated sugar

1 teaspoon (5 mL) salt

1 1/2 teaspoons (7 mL) instant yeast

3/4 cup (175 mL) hot water (130°F/55°C)

1 tablespoon (15 mL) oil

1 egg

2 teaspoons (10 mL) soft butter

1/2 cup (125 mL) brown sugar

1 teaspoon (5 mL) cinnamon

1/2 cup (125 mL) raisins or currants

icing:

1 tablespoon (15 mL) soft butter

1 tablespoon (15 mL) milk

1 cup approx. (250 mL) icing sugar

Christmas Bread

When Marg Routledge, of Fredericton, NB, shared with us her recipe for Christmas Bread, she had this to say:

"For nearly 20 years I have made several breads for our parish church craft sale in November. These are baked the morning of the sale, decorated and wrapped like Christmas presents, ready to put into the freezer until Christmas morning. We have regular customers who line up before the doors open, and the breads are sold out within 10 minutes."

Marg is no stranger to Atlantic cooks. She is a home economist and food consultant who, with Donna Young, wrote New Maritimes Seasonal Cooking *(Firefly Books, 1999), which includes delicious recipes for light and healthy meals year round.*

In large bowl, mix 1 cup (250 mL) of the flour, sugar, salt and yeast. Stir in hot water and oil. Add egg and beat until mixture is smooth and elastic. Mix in enough of remaining flour to make a soft dough. Turn on floured surface and knead 5 minutes. Return to bowl, cover and let rise in warm place until double in bulk, 1 hour.

Punch down, let rest 5 minutes. Roll a 24x12-inch (60x30 cm) rectangle. Spread with soft butter and sprinkle with brown sugar, cinnamon, and raisins or currants. Roll up jelly roll fashion, starting at long edge.

For wreath shape: Bring ends together and pinch to form circle. Carefully lift ring onto oiled cookie sheet, forming even circle with seam down. Use scissors to cut halfway through the dough at 1-inch (2.5 cm) intervals. Twist each piece so that cinnamon rings are exposed and the dough resembles a wreath.

For Christmas tree: Cut the roll into 16 pieces. Place pieces, with cinnamon rings exposed, in shape of tree on an oiled cookie sheet. The last roll forms the tree trunk. Leave space between rolls for them to rise and give tree shape.

Cover with tea towel and let rise in a warm place until double in size. Bake at 350°F (180°C) until golden, 15 to 20 minutes.

Icing: Make butter icing by beating together butter, milk, and enough icing sugar to make a soft icing. Cool bread on wire rack. When slightly warm, drizzle icing over top; decorate with red and green cherries and toasted almonds. Makes 16 servings.

Tip:

If you have a bread machine with a dough option, this recipe will work; add the dough ingredients as listed to bread pan and pick up the directions after the first rising.

Cranberry Lemon Loaf

Cranberries are grown on bogs in Atlantic Canada. They may be available fresh to local consumers through January, but lovers of this piquant berry will stock up by tossing a few extra bags into their freezers. From these you can create, along with sauces and desserts, a parade of tasty breads and muffins. For best texture and flavour, this bread should be made a day before serving.

Sift together flour, baking powder and salt; set aside. In mixer bowl, cream together butter and sugar until light and fluffy. Add eggs, one at a time, beating well after each addition. Add lemon rind; mix well. Add dry ingredients alternately with milk; beat until smooth. Fold in cranberries and nuts.

Pour batter into a greased 9x5x3-inch (23x13x6 cm) pan. Bake at 350°F (180°C) for 55 to 60 minutes, or until a toothpick inserted in centre comes out clean. Cool in pan 10 minutes before turning out onto a rack to cool completely. Makes one loaf.

Topping: Combine sugar and lemon juice; spoon over top.

ingredients

- 2 cups (500 mL) all-purpose flour
- 2 1/2 teaspoons (12 mL) baking powder
- 1 teaspoon (5 mL) salt, or less, to taste
- 4 tablespoons (60 mL) softened butter
- 3/4 cup (175 mL) granulated sugar
- 2 eggs
- 2 teaspoons (10 mL) grated lemon rind
- 3/4 cup (175 mL) milk
- 1 cup (250 mL) fresh cranberries, chopped
- 1/2 cup (125 mL) chopped walnuts or pecans

topping:

- 2 tablespoons (30 mL) sugar
- 2 teaspoons (10 mL) lemon juice

ingredients

- 2 cups (500 mL) all-purpose flour
- 2 1/2 teaspoons (12 mL) baking powder
- 1 teaspoon (5 mL) salt
- 1/2 teaspoon (2 mL) ground cinnamon
- 1/2 teaspoon (2 mL) ground allspice
- 1/4 teaspoon (1 mL) grated nutmeg
- 3/4 cup (175 mL) granulated sugar
- 1/3 cup (75 mL) canola oil
- 2 eggs
- 1 1/4 cups (300 mL) canned pumpkin (not pumpkin pie filling)
- 1/2 cup (125 mL) milk
- 2 cups (500 mL) fresh or frozen cranberries, chopped (do not thaw, if frozen)
- 1/2 cup (125 mL) chopped walnuts

Cranberry Pumpkin Muffins

There are foods that just naturally go together, and these products of the fall harvest get my vote for a delicious pairing. By stretching it a bit, a large can of pumpkin (28 ounce/796 mL) is enough to make 3 batches of muffins, which can be stockpiled in the freezer for early morning breakfasts, or snacks during the day.

Sift dry ingredients together; set aside. In mixer bowl, combine oil, eggs, pumpkin and milk. Stir in dry ingredients just until moistened. Do not over-mix. Fold in cranberries and nuts.

Fill 12 well-greased medium muffin cups 2/3 full. Bake in a preheated 400°F (200°C) oven for 20 to 25 minutes, or until muffins are golden in colour and spring back when lightly pressed. Let cool for a few minutes before turning out on a rack. Serve warm. Makes 12 muffins.

Make a Christmas Wreath

Bring nature to your door

1 Begin by collecting evergreen "tips"— pieces of evergreen branches that are between 14 and 16 inches long. (Make sure you ask permission from landowners before tipping trees.)

Using wire cutters or gardening shears, trim these "tips" into hand-sized pieces.

2 Pile three or four small pieces together to create "hands" or "palms" of greenery that will be wired to the wreath form. Work proceeds quickly if you have several "hands" prepared at a time.

3 Attach one end of your floral wire to the wreath frame. Hold a "palm" of greenery in place on the front of the wire wreath frame. Wind the floral wire around the end of the boughs and the frame. A couple of twists should secure the palm in place.

Do not cut the floral wire, you will be using one continuous length of wire to secure all the palms to the wreath form. Place a second palm of greenery on the back of the frame, a few inches farther along the wreath form. Secure it in place with the floral wire.

4 Secure a third palm of greenery on the front, overlapping the first, a fourth on the back, overlapping the second and so on. The fullness of your wreath will be determined by how closely you place the palms and the number of pieces in each palm. Proceed along the wreath form, layering your palms.

5 Secure the final palm with an extra wind and cut floral wire. Insert small pieces of greenery beneath wire to fill out this area.

6 Trim uneven pieces of greenery with wire cutters. Decorate with berries, pine cones, ribbons or other items.

Tips for making your wreath

Wreath making can be a messy process, thanks to falling needles. Build your wreath in a basement, garage, barn or some other place that can easily be swept out.

Wear old clothes. Evergreen boughs can be gummy.

Do not use large, unwieldy pieces. Cut boughs into palm-sized "hands." If you are looking for a fuller wreath, use four pieces of greenery per "hand" instead of three.

For a wreath that will lie flat against a door, cover only the front side of the wreath form.

appetizers and beverages

Holiday time is a time for entertaining friends and relatives, and whether it's a sit-down dinner or a casual gathering over the cocktail hour, the well-prepared host will have appetizers and beverages ready.

A little—or a lot—of advance planning can take the stress out of a party that even the hosts will enjoy. Decisions should be made early as to what kind of a party is right for you. If your space is small, an open house with staggered hours might be the answer. It's a good time to invite compatible friends for an elegant meal, if you can handle it, or a casual supper, if you can't. If time and energy are on the short side, a "grazing" party, with an assortment of prepared finger foods from the deli, might be the answer.

But whichever way you go (except, of course, for the elegant dinner party) it's best at this time of year to keep things simple.

A list of what needs to be done and a timetable to do it all will keep you organized and relaxed. Take advantage of your freezer. This is no time for last-minute food preparation.

Of course, there will be drinks, which also need advance planning. Assess your crowd and order accordingly. But, whether it will be punch, wine, alcohol, or some of each, there is one further decision to make: there must be at least one non-alcoholic choice. That could simply be a mixture of tomato or vegetable juice and soda water, with a little added lemon juice to perk it up (48 ounces/1.5 L of juice and 10 ounces/300 mL of soda water will make seven 1-cup/250-mL servings). Or, if the weather outside is frightful, what better offering could there be than a mug of hot cranberry lemonade?

Baked Brie with Cranberry Chutney

For this delicious appetizer, choose an ovenproof dish that fits the cheese closely.

If using small cheese rounds, 2 ramekins work well. For easy removal of rind, place brie in the freezer for 30 minutes. Butter the dish or ramekins; set aside.

Prepare chutney: In a medium saucepan over medium-high heat, bring to a boil the cranberries, sugar, vinegar, water, ginger, cinnamon and cloves. Reduce heat to low and simmer for about 20 minutes, or until mixture thickens. Cool. (Chutney can be made ahead, cooled, covered and refrigerated for up to a week, or it can be frozen for up to a month.)

When ready to bake, trim top rind from brie. Place brie in prepared dish and bake in a 350°F (180°C) oven for 15 to 20 minutes, or until cheese has softened and just started to melt. Be careful not to over-bake. Remove from oven, spoon chutney over cheese, and serve with crackers. Makes 8 to 10 servings.

ingredients

1 (8 ounce/250 g) round brie

1 cup (250 mL) fresh or
   frozen cranberries

2/3 cup (150 mL) granulated sugar

1/3 cup (75 mL) cider vinegar

2 tablespoons (30 mL) water

2 teaspoons (10 mL) grated fresh
   gingerroot

1/4 teaspoon (1 mL) ground cinnamon

1/8 teaspoon (0.5 mL) ground cloves

Crab Grass (the good kind)

Cook spinach according to package directions; drain thoroughly, squeezing out excess moisture. Set aside. Melt butter in a heavy saucepan over medium-low heat. Add onion and sauté until limp. Add garlic, if using, during the last few seconds of cooking (overcooking destroys the flavour and browning makes it bitter). Stir in spinach, then crabmeat and parmesan.

This is best served in a chafing dish to keep it warm. Serve with tortilla chips or an assortment of crackers. Makes about 3 cups (750 mL).

To make tortilla chips: Cut 8-inch flour tortillas into 12 wedges, place them in a single layer on a baking sheet, and bake in a 350°F (180°C) oven for about 8 minutes, until they just start to brown. Cool and serve with Crab Grass (the good kind).

Tip:

To celebrate in fine style, what could be better than a taste of champagne? To pick up on the green of the holiday season, pour a little Creme de Menthe into a chilled champagne flute, and gently pour in the champagne or sparkling wine. Do not stir, allowing the bubbles to do their work.

ingredients

1 (10 oz/300 g) package frozen chopped spinach

1/2 cup (125 mL) butter

1/2 cup (125 mL) chopped onion

1 clove garlic, minced (optional)

1 cup (250 mL) chopped crabmeat

3/4 cup (175 mL) grated parmesan cheese

Salt and pepper to taste

Tortilla chips or crackers

ingredients

1 pound (500 g) fresh mushrooms

1/2 cup (125 mL) butter or margarine

6 tablespoons (90 mL) flour

1 teaspoon (5 mL) salt

2 cups (500 mL) light cream

1 tablespoon (15 mL) minced chives

2 teaspoons (10 mL) lemon juice

2 sandwich loaves white bread

Melted butter

Toasted Mushroom Rolls

During the holidays, it's handy to have a good supply of appetizers in the freezer ready to heat and serve when guests arrive. These easy-to-make mushroom rolls are among my favourites.

Wipe mushrooms with damp paper towels; cut into small dice. Sauté in butter for 5 minutes. Blend in flour and salt. Stir in cream and simmer until thickened. Add chives and lemon juice.

Remove crusts from bread. Roll each slice with a rolling pin to prevent cracking. Spread thin layer of mushroom mixture almost to edges of bread. Roll up. Place in single layers in containers and freeze until ready to serve.

Before serving, cut each roll in half and brush with melted butter. Defrost and bake at 450°F (230°C) for 10 to 15 minutes. Makes 70 to 80 rolls.

Asian Meatballs

These meatballs can be made ahead, cooked, cooled, and frozen for up to three months. To serve, thaw and heat in the microwave or wrap in foil and reheat in the oven.

In a large bowl, lightly combine all ingredients (over-mixing will toughen the meatballs). Form mixture into about 30 (1-inch/2.5 cm) balls. Place on a lightly oiled rimmed baking sheet and bake, without turning, in a preheated 400°F (200°C) oven for 15 minutes. (A digital rapid-read thermometer inserted in centre of a meatball should read 160°F [71°C]). Serve with sweet and sour or plum sauce. Makes about 30 meatballs.

ingredients

1 pound (500 g) lean ground beef

1 egg, lightly beaten

1/2 cup (125 mL) dry bread crumbs

1/3 cup (75 mL) finely grated carrot

1/3 cup (75 mL) finely chopped green onion

2 tablespoons (30 mL) hoisin sauce

1 tablespoon (15 mL) Worcestershire sauce

1/2 teaspoon (2 mL) ground ginger

1/2 teaspoon (2 mL) salt

1/2 teaspoon (2 mL) pepper

Hazelnut Chicken Bites with Pineapple Mustard Sauce

Made with real chicken, these delicious and easy-to-make appetizers are a hit with young and old. But I warn you, they're addictive. And you'll never be happy again with those pressed chicken pieces that promise more than they deliver.

Cut chicken into 1-inch (2.5 cm) pieces. In a small bowl, mix together breadcrumbs, nuts, and seasonings. In another bowl, beat together egg and water. Lightly dust chicken pieces in flour; dip in egg mixture, and then in crumbs.

Place coated bites on an ungreased, nonstick baking pan. Bake at 425°F (220°C) about 15 minutes, until chicken is tender and cooked through.

Sauce: In small saucepan, combine pineapple with juice, sugar, mustard and horseradish. Stirring occasionally, simmer over medium heat until thickened, about 10 minutes. Serve bites with sauce. Makes about 32 bites.

ingredients

1 pound (500 g) boneless chicken breasts

1/2 cup (125 mL) fine dry breadcrumbs

1/2 cup (125 mL) finely chopped hazelnuts or pecans

1/2 teaspoon (2 mL) garlic powder

1/4 teaspoon (1 mL) paprika

Salt and freshly ground pepper to taste

1 egg

1 tablespoon (15 mL) water

Flour, for dusting

sauce:

1/2 cup (125 mL) crushed pineapple with juice

1 tablespoon (15 mL) granulated sugar

2 tablespoons (30 mL) coarse grained mustard

2 tablespoons (30 mL) horseradish

Cottage Cheese and Spinach Cups

Don't let the spinach fool you. I have served these appetizers to very finicky eaters and, even if dubious at first, they're always pleasantly surprised, and invariably reach for another.

Spoon cottage cheese into a strainer, drain well, and set aside.

Thaw chopped spinach in a colander until well drained; press or squeeze as much moisture out of spinach as possible.

In a bowl, mix together the drained cottage cheese, spinach, beaten eggs, salt, pepper and nutmeg. Combine well. Spoon 2 teaspoons (10 mL) of mixture into each pastry shell; bake at 350°F (180°C) for 25 to 30 minutes, or until set. Makes about 6 dozen appetizers.

ingredients

1 1/2 cups (375 mL) cottage cheese

2 (10 ounce/300 g) packages frozen chopped spinach, thawed

4 eggs, beaten

1/2 teaspoon (2 mL) salt

1/4 teaspoon (1 mL) pepper

1/4 teaspoon (1 mL) ground nutmeg

Miniature Cream Cheese Pastry Shells (recipe follows)

Miniature Cream Cheese Pastry Shells

Combine flour and salt. Cut in cream cheese and butter until mixture resembles coarse crumbs. Press mixture together with hands until it forms a dough.

Shape dough into 72 (1 inch/2.5 cm) balls. Place each ball into an ungreased 1 3/4 inch (4.5 cm) muffin cup. Press dough onto bottom and sides to form shells. Makes about 6 dozen shells.

ingredients

3 cups (750 mL) all-purpose flour

1/4 teaspoon (1 mL) salt

1 (8-ounce/250 g) package cream cheese, softened

1 cup (250 mL) butter

Marinated Broccoli and Honey Dip

Nothing could be easier to prepare than this make-ahead appetizer that gives a festive air to bright green broccoli, scattered with bits of red pimento. The broccoli can be cut up a day ahead and left to marinate in the fridge for hours. And the dip can be made in less than 2 minutes.

Break broccoli into florets and cut into bite-sized pieces. In a large sealable plastic bag, combine vinegar, oil, garlic, sugar and dill weed. Add broccoli, seal tightly and place in refrigerator to marinate for several hours. Drain well.

Place drained broccoli in a serving dish and scatter chopped pimento over it. Serve with Honey Dip. Makes about 20 servings.

Honey Dip: In a jar with a tight-fitting cover, combine honey, vinegar, mustard, garlic and oil. Cover and shake well to mix. Pour into a serving bowl to accompany Marinated Broccoli.

ingredients

1 large head broccoli

1/4 cup (50 mL) white wine vinegar

3/4 cup (175 mL) canola oil

2 cloves garlic, minced

1 teaspoon (5 mL) sugar

2 teaspoons (10 mL) dill weed

Garnish: Chopped pimento

honey dip:

1/4 cup (50 mL) liquid honey

3 tablespoons (45 mL) white wine vinegar

2 tablespoons (30 mL) coarse grain brown mustard

1 clove garlic, minced

1/2 cup (125 mL) canola oil

Zucchini and Walnut Spread

Keep your guests guessing at the main ingredient of this spread. I'll bet they almost never catch on. Nor would they believe how easy it is to prepare.

Sprinkle zucchini with 2 teaspoons (10 mL) salt, tossing well. Place in a colander and let drain over the sink for 30 minutes. Squeeze dry in a clean tea towel.

Combine oil, vinegar, garlic, and pepper in a blender and pulse to mix. Add the drained zucchini and blend until smooth, scraping down the sides occasionally. Season with salt, if needed. Cover and refrigerate for up to 2 days. Fold in the walnuts just before serving. Serve in a bowl, surrounded by crackers. Makes 2 1/2 cups (625 mL).

ingredients

5 cups (1.25 L) coarsely shredded zucchini

2 teaspoons (10 mL) salt

1/4 cup (50 mL) canola oil

1 tablespoon (15 mL) red wine or cider vinegar

1 clove garlic, minced

Freshly ground black pepper, to taste

1/2 cup (125 mL) finely chopped walnuts

Danish Coffee

Serve coffee in a cup and place a small piece of bittersweet chocolate on the saucer. Nibble off a tiny piece of chocolate, and with your tongue, tuck it behind your lower teeth. Sip the coffee through it and envision heaven.

Frangelica Coffee

To a cup of strong black coffee, add a good-sized piece of bittersweet chocolate. Stir in a good dose of Frangelica liqueur, and you've found the perfect threesome.

Hot Chococoff

Thermal coffee servers are perfect for this beverage. You'll need two (borrow one, or both, if you have to). Fill one thermos with freshly brewed coffee, the other with hot chocolate. Let guests help themselves by filling their cups or mugs with equal portions of each beverage. You might also want to provide a bowl of whipped cream and chocolate sprinkles for garnish.

Rum Eggnog

Start preparing this eggnog half an hour before your guests arrive. It's important to have all the ingredients and bowls as cold as possible. A pretty punch bowl and cups to serve it in adds a festive touch, but chilled old-fashioned glasses make a nice alternative. Freshly grated nutmeg rings in the good cheer.

In large mixer bowl, beat egg yolks until thick and light. Gradually add sugar and beat well. Transfer to another large bowl (to free your mixer bowl for whipping the cream). Add brandy and rum, a little at a time, stirring constantly.

Thoroughly wash mixer bowl and beaters. Whip cream and fold into yolk mixture.

Once again, clean the bowl and beaters. Rapidly beat egg whites with salt until fluffy. Fold whites into yolk mixture. Add milk. Pour into punch bowl and sprinkle generously with freshly grated nutmeg. Serve immediately or keep refrigerated until needed. Makes at least 50 servings.

ingredients

12 eggs, separated

1 cup (250 mL) granulated sugar

1/2 cup (125 mL) brandy

2 cups (500 mL) rum

4 cups (1 L) whipping cream

Pinch of salt

2 cups (500 mL) milk

Nutmeg

Holiday Red Wine Punch

You can make this bowl of cheer with or without the wine. If making it a non-alcoholic drink, replace the wine with ginger ale.

In a large bowl, combine cranberry cocktail, lemonade and grenadine. Pour into two containers, such as gallon (4 L) plastic ice cream containers, and store in the refrigerator until well chilled.

Just before serving time, combine, pour one container of punch base into a punch bowl. Pour in one bottle of red wine, stir to combine. Add ice cubes or ice ring. Garnish with half-slices of orange, lemon or lime or a mixture of all three.

When supplies run low, repeat procedure with remaining base and wine. Makes 30 (5-ounce/155-mL) drinks with ice.

ingredients

6 cups (1.5 L) cranberry cocktail

1 (355 mL) container frozen lemonade, thawed

1/2 cup (125 mL) grenadine

2 (1.5 L) bottles dry red wine

Ice cubes or ice ring

Tia "Marie"

A friend gave me this recipe many years ago and I immediately adopted it as my own. Tia "Marie" became the house liqueur and nobody seemed to notice a difference between this and the real thing.

ingredients

2 cups (500 mL) water

1-inch (2.5 cm) length of vanilla bean, cut into 3 pieces

3 3/4 cups (925 mL) granulated sugar

4 1/2 tablespoons (67 mL) instant coffee

1/2 cup (125 mL) warm water

1 (750 mL) bottle vodka

1 teaspoon (5 mL) glycerine

In large saucepan, put 2 cups (500 mL) water, vanilla bean and sugar. Stir over moderate heat until sugar dissolves. Bring to a boil and continue boiling gently for 30 minutes. Set aside to cool.

Dissolve coffee granules in 1/2 cup (125 mL) warm water. Add to cooled sugar syrup. Strain three times through cheese cloth into large bowl. Pour in vodka and glycerine. Stir well. Pour through funnel into two liqueur or liquor bottles. Cap well. Shake and allow to stand 2 weeks before using. Makes about 2 quarts (2 L).

soups and chowders

Saltscapes was just a year old when it launched its first comfort food recipe contest. Could such a baby handle the Herculean task of choosing 7 winners from among the 397 recipes so enthusiastically entered? We could and we did. The categories were a perfect fit for Atlantic Canadians. Who better to prepare the best seafood chowders and toss in a few soups for good tasting? And who better to bake the breads that have become a benchmark for this part of the world? No one.

Still, a recipe contest is only as good as its entries, and our readers proved they were up to the task, making it most difficult for the judges to single out a grand prize winner.

But they did it, and the unanimous choice was Philip Theriault of Chester, NS. His favourite chowder is a meal in itself, jam-packed with all the wonderful shellfish from these waters—lobster, scallops, clams, and mussels, along with a few jumbo shrimp, borrowed from another seacoast location. The recipe is included here, along with another winning seafood chowder, developed by Austin Clement, of Charlottetown, PEI.

When Atlantic Canadians say "chowder," they most often mean seafood chowder, whether it is a single shellfish, such as clams, lobster or oysters, or a mixture of shellfish and finfish. With winners such as these, a whole new world of gastronomy is contained within the next two pages, just waiting to be enjoyed by chowder connoisseurs.

To be good—or better—soups and chowders could contain an often-tossed-away ingredient: the water in which your vegetables are cooked. What a shame when all those nutrients are poured down the sink when they might be adding richness to another meal.

Philip's Favourite Seafood Chowder

This wonderful chowder was the grand prize winner in Saltscapes's first Comfort Food Recipe Contest (2001). It is the creation of Philip Theriault, of Chester, NS, who said, "The key point to remember is to sauté the seafood gently in butter and not to overcook it. And the longer the chowder sits after being mixed, the more flavourful it will be."

Prepare seafood: remove meat from lobster, cut into bite-sized pieces. Leave scallops whole. Peel raw shrimp. Wipe haddock, if using, and cut into bite-sized pieces. Place clams and mussels in water to soak; remove beards from mussels. Place all seafood in fridge until needed.

In a stockpot, cook potatoes and onions in enough water to keep them from sticking, for about 12 to 15 minutes. They should be just barely cooked (still crunchy). Remove from heat and lay haddock (if using) on top. Cover pot and set aside.

Using half of the butter, gently sauté lobster over low heat just until a reddish sauce is formed. Do not overcook or the lobster will be tough. Add scallops and shrimp and sauté for one minute more. Remove from heat; keep warm.

Drain potato mixture. Add evaporated milk and enough milk or cream to make desired thickness. Gently stir in seafood and butter sauce. Add a little extra milk to the sauté pan; scrape and add to pot. Add bay leaves; gently simmer until potatoes are fully cooked and flavours blend. Add remaining butter and stir when melted. Season to taste with salt and pepper. Stir in parsley.

Just before serving, steam clams and mussels until shells open, about 2 to 3 minutes. Remove bay leaves. Ladle chowder into a serving dish or individual bowls. Sprinkle with chopped parsley and cayenne. Arrange shellfish (in shell) around edge of bowl on top of chowder. Serve with crusty bread. Makes 4 servings.

ingredients

Meat from 1 cooked lobster

4 to 8 ounces (125 to 250 g) fresh scallops

6 to 8 raw jumbo shrimp (if using cooked shrimp, add just before serving)

1 small haddock fillet, cut into bite-sized pieces (optional)

6 fresh clams, in shells

6 fresh mussels, in shells

4 to 5 medium potatoes, cubed

2 medium onions, diced

2 to 3 tablespoons (30 to 45 mL) butter

1 can (385 mL) evaporated milk

Light cream or whole milk to thicken

2 bay leaves

Salt and freshly ground pepper, to taste

2 tablespoons (30 mL) chopped parsley, or to taste

Garnish: cayenne pepper and chopped parsley

ingredients

8 ounces (250 g) lobster meat

8 ounces (250 g) cooked scallops

8 ounces (250 g) cooked haddock,
cut in large dice

8 ounces (250 g) cooked shrimp,
cut in medium dice

8 ounces (250 g) cooked mussel meat,
left whole

4 cups (1 L) fish stock (used to poach
the fish)

2 bay leaves

2 star anise pods

3 peppercorns

3 parsley stems

1/3 cup (75 mL) butter

1 cup (250 mL) chopped onion

1 cup (250 mL) chopped celery

1/2 cup (125 mL) chopped sweet red pepper

1/2 cup (125 mL) flour

4 cups (1 L) potatoes, cut in medium dice

4 cups (1 L) heavy cream, scalded

Salt and white pepper, to taste

Austin's Maritime Seafood Chowder

Austin Clement, a chef instructor at the Culinary Institute of Canada, Charlottetown, PEI, is quite used to taking bows with his multiple prize-winning seafood chowder recipe. He's been making it for several years and sees no reason to change it. Any white fish works well in this chowder, but he advises against stirring too much after the fish is added, or it will break up and lose its texture.

Poach all seafood in fish stock for about 2 minutes until it is just cooked; set aside, but keep warm. Make a sachet from bay leaves, star anise, peppercorns and parsley; set aside.

In a heavy-bottomed 6-quart (6 L) pot, melt butter, add onions, celery and peppers and cook until limp. Add flour and cook to make a blond roux. Gradually add fish stock, whisking to work out any lumps. Bring to a simmer. Add the sachet and cook for 10 minutes. Add potatoes and continue to simmer until potatoes are tender, about 15 minutes. Add scalded cream and seafood and stir just to combine. Simmer 5 minutes more. Remove and discard the sachet and adjust seasoning with salt and pepper. Let sit for 20 minutes. Check seasoning one last time. Serve. Makes 8 servings.

Turkey Scotch Broth

When the turkey is all, as they say in Lunenburg County, there is still the carcass from which to gain one last meal. It takes time to pull the flavour and nourishment from the bones, but it is well worth the effort, and the pot needs little watching. If your appetite for turkey is a bit jaded, you can freeze the soup to enjoy a month or two later.

Dismember turkey carcass, pulling off scraps of meat and setting them aside. Put carcass into a large soup pot, along with other unusable leftovers and pan scrapings. The pot may be refrigerated until the next day. Refrigerate or freeze scraps of meat.

To make broth, add about 10 cups of boiling water, or enough to cover solids. Bring to a gentle boil, then simmer gently, partly covered, for 4 hours or more. Strain broth into a bowl and refrigerate overnight, or until fat hardens and can be lifted off with a spoon. Discard carcass.

To make Scotch Broth, remove congealed fat and heat stock to boiling. Add barley, carrots, celery and onion. Simmer, partly covered, for 1 hour and 45 minutes. Add parsley and cook 15 minutes longer. Taste and correct seasoning, adding no more than 1/4 teaspoon (1 mL) at a time. Stir in reserved turkey scraps and bring to simmer. Makes 10 servings.

ingredients

1 turkey carcass

1/2 cup (125 mL) barley

2 medium carrots, chopped

2 ribs celery, chopped

1 medium onion, chopped

1/4 cup (50 mL) fresh parsley, chopped

Salt and pepper, to taste

main courses

For many Atlantic Canadians, the big feast of the holiday season simply must centre around a roast turkey with the kind of stuffing that has been the family favourite through several generations. Nothing must change.

In other homes, a few modern trends may gradually creep in to meld with the old, giving birth to a whole new set of traditions, customized to a family's preferences. If that family prefers a potato dressing over bread, or are anxious to try an oyster or sausage stuffing, what is holding them back? Call them free-thinking adventurers. For them, turkey, served on both Thanksgiving and Christmas or Hanukkah, has become boring by New Year's. Mouths water for a prime rib of beef, a thick slice of good ham, or even a helping of the Down East specialty, seafood casserole.

One Newfoundlander from St. John's spoke of the long-standing Christmas meal served in the home in which he grew up with his parents and 11 siblings. Yes, there was a huge turkey, but there was also a roast of beef and a large ham—all for the same meal.

Couples, especially seniors, may opt for roast chicken in order to escape endless meals of leftovers, while the chief cook in larger families may actually plan for extras in order to be inventive the second and third time 'round.

Turkey with Dressing

Before cooking a turkey, you must decide what to buy. As a guide, a 14-pound (about 7 kg) turkey will serve six people, an 18-pound (about 9 kg) will serve eight and a 22-pounder (about 11 kg) will feed ten to twelve people. With all sizes there should be leftovers for the next day. Make sure your refrigerator can handle the turkey you buy, since a fresh turkey must be refrigerated until cooking time and a frozen bird should thaw in the fridge.

how long to cook a turkey

Weight		Oven times at 325°F (160°C)	
Pounds	**Kilograms**	**Stuffed**	**Unstuffed**
6–8	3–3.5	3–3 1/4 hrs.	2 1/2–2 3/4 hrs.
8–10	3.5–4.5	3 1/4–3 1/2 hrs.	2 3/4 - 3 hrs.
10–12	4.5–5.5	3 1/2–3 3/4 hrs.	3–3 1/4 hrs.
12–16	5.5–7.0	3 3/–4 hrs.	3 1/4–3 1/2 hrs.
16–22	7.0–10	4–4 1/2 hrs.	3 1/2–4 hrs.

To prepare the turkey for cooking, examine the body cavity for any unpalatable parts, such as the lungs or windpipe, and remove them. Run your hand over the skin, feeling for hair and pin feathers. Pin feathers may be removed with tweezers and hair may be singed with a lighted match. Be sure to remove the giblet bag, which is often found in the neck cavity.

Rinse and dry the bird thoroughly before stuffing it. Sprinkle both the neck and body cavity with salt and then loosely pack in the stuffing, bearing in mind that it will expand during cooking.

Although stuffing ingredients may be prepared early and stored in separate containers in the refrigerator, they should not be combined until the bird is almost ready for the oven. A bird should never be stuffed ahead since bacteria can grow quickly in this environment.

After trussing the turkey, place it on a rack in an open roasting pan. Rub it with oil. Cover it with a loose tent of aluminum foil (making sure the thighs and neck are well shielded) and roast at 325°F (160°C) according to the time table below.

Remove the aluminum foil during the last half hour of roasting in order to brown the turkey nicely. It's at this time that a meat thermometer should be inserted into the centre of the stuffing for about 5 minutes. The turkey is done when the stuffing temperature reaches 165°F (74°C), the drumstick and breast meat feel soft and the leg moves easily when twisted. The juices should run clear.

The cooked turkey should not be allowed to stand at room temperature for more than 2 hours. Dressing should be removed and stored separately. The leftover meat generally may be stored, covered, in the refrigerator for 3 to 4 days.

Basic Bread Stuffing

Since heat brings out the flavour of summer savoury, it's hard to gauge how much to use. It's better to add too little than too much. But make a note on the recipe so next time you'll know how much to use for your family's tastes.

Melt butter in a skillet. Sauté onions and celery for about 5 minutes.

In a large bowl, combine bread cubes, summer savoury, salt and pepper. Add onion mixture and enough stock to make stuffing hold together when squeezed between thumb and index finger.

ingredients

(Enough for a 10-12 pound/5-6 kg turkey)

1/4 cup (50 mL) butter

2 onions, chopped

2 ribs celery, chopped

8 cups (2 L) cubed slightly stale bread (1/2 inch/1 cm cubes)

1/2 to 1 teaspoon (2 to 5 mL) dried summer savoury, or to taste

1/2 teaspoon (2 mL) salt

1/4 teaspoon (1 mL) pepper

1/3 to 1/2 cup (75 to 125 mL) chicken stock or water

Prime Rib au Jus

Coarsely chop garlic cloves. Using the side of a chef's knife, mash the garlic and salt together on a cutting board, using circular motions until paste-like. Combine with rosemary, pepper, mustard and oil. Rub all over roast.

Place roast, fat-side-up, on a rack in a roasting pan. Insert meat thermometer into centre of roast, avoiding fat and bone. Cook uncovered, in a 325°F (160°C) oven to desired doneness (see below). Remove roast to cutting board; tent with foil for 10 to 15 minutes to allow temperature to rise by 5°F (3°C). Using a gentle sawing action, carve roast into thick slices across the grain.

Makes 10 generous servings.

Au Jus: In roasting pan, skim off any fat from cooking juices; place pan over medium-high heat. Stir in 1 to 2 cups (250–500 mL) beef stock or broth and bring to a boil, stirring up any browned bits from bottom of pan. Reduce heat to medium and continue cooking until sauce is reduced and becomes slightly thickened. Strain if you like and season to taste.

Au Jus Options: Add 1/4 cup (50 mL) dry red wine and/or 1 teaspoon (5 mL) chopped fresh rosemary or thyme to the beef stock before bringing to a boil. To finish the sauce, try adding a splash of balsamic vinegar or heavy cream, if desired.

Yorkshire Pudding

Could anything be more festive to serve with a prime roast of beef than Yorkshire Pudding? Prepare the batter ahead, refrigerate, and bring to room temperature an hour before proceeding.

In a bowl, combine 1 cup (250 mL) flour and 1/4 teaspoon (1 mL) salt. In another bowl, beat together 1 egg and 1 1/4 cups (300 mL) milk. Make a well in flour and pour in egg mixture. Beat at medium speed until smooth, then beat 2 minutes at high speed. (Can be made ahead to this point and refrigerated. Take from fridge 1 hour before proceeding.)

Pour 1/2 teaspoon (2 mL) pan drippings into 8 large muffin cups. Place in a 450°F (230°C) oven for 2 minutes. Divide batter equally into hot muffin cups. Return to oven immediately and bake 15 to 20 minutes, until puffy and golden and serve at once with roast beef. Makes 8 Yorkshire puddings.

---

ingredients

5 garlic cloves

1 teaspoon (5 mL) salt

1 tablespoon (15 mL) chopped fresh rosemary or thyme (or 1 teaspoon/ 5 mL dried)

1/2 teaspoon (2 mL) pepper

1/2 teaspoon (2 mL) grainy Dijon mustard

1 tablespoon (15 mL) canola oil

8 pounds (3.5 kg) bone-in prime rib premium oven roast

Tips

- For restaurant-size portions, purchase 12 ounces (375 g) per person for bone-in prime rib. For a boneless prime rib, allow 6 to 8 ounces (150–250 g) per person.

- For easy carving, ask your butcher or meat counter staff to cut the prime rib meat from the ribs and then have them tied back on. The bones will add flavour while roasting and they can be easily removed when carving with just a snip of the string.

- Butchers tie the roast across the grain—just cut parallel to the butcher twine to cut across the grain.

- When carving, set cutting board into a rimmed baking sheet to collect juices.

Doneness

RARE MEAT – Cook 20 min per lb/500 g.

Internal temperature when removed from oven should be 135°F (57°C).

MEDIUM MEAT – Cook 25 min per lb/500 g.

Internal temperature when removed from oven should be 155°F (68°C).

WELL DONE MEAT – Cook 30 min per lb/500 g.

Internal temperature when removed from oven should be 165°F (72°C).

Roast Chicken with Maple Walnut Stuffing

Rinse chickens inside and out, and pat dry. Lightly season with salt and pepper.

In a large saucepan, heat butter and oil. Add chopped onion and celery, and cook until limp, about 5 minutes. Add bread cubes, walnuts, maple syrup, summer savoury, salt and pepper. Toss to combine. (If dressing is too dry add a tablespoon or two [15–30 mL] of water, just enough to make the stuffing hold together when squeezed between thumb and forefinger.)

Loosely fill neck and cavity of chickens with stuffing. Close openings and tie legs tightly together. Place breast side up in a shallow roasting pan, leaving a little space between chickens. Rub all over with melted butter or oil. Cover birds loosely with foil, and roast in a preheated 450°F (230°C) oven for 10 minutes. Reduce heat to 350°F (180°C) and continue roasting for 30 minutes. Remove foil and brush with maple syrup. Roast uncovered for another 30 minutes, or until chickens test done, brushing a couple of times with maple syrup.

Test for doneness: Thighs should feel soft when pressed, and juices should run clear, with no sign of pink. Let stand 15 minutes before carving. Makes 6 to 8 servings.

Tip:

To toast walnuts, spread evenly in a shallow pan and bake at 350°F (180°C) until lightly browned, 5 to 7 minutes. Watch carefully; they burn easily.

ingredients

2 (2 1/2 to 3 pound/1 to 1.5 kg) chickens

Salt and pepper

Melted butter or oil

stuffing

2 tablespoons (30 mL) butter

2 tablespoons (30 mL) canola oil

1 small onion, chopped

1 celery rib, chopped

4 cups (1 L) slightly stale bread cubes

1/2 cup (125 mL) toasted chopped walnuts (see tip)

1/4 cup (50 mL) maple syrup

1 teaspoon (5 mL) summer savoury, or more to taste

Salt and pepper to taste

Maple syrup for basting

Baked Ham Slice with Cherry Sauce

If you're planning a New Year's Eve buffet and you've already looked too many turkeys in the eye, choose ham as a colourful and tasty alternative. A tender and meaty centre slice of a fully cooked bone-in ham, cut about 2 1/2 inches (6 cm) thick, can serve 8 to 10 people, with enough left over for sandwiches.

A mustard sauce, made by heating 1/2 cup (125 mL) each of prepared mustard and red currant jelly makes a nice option to the cherry sauce.

If ham has a layer of fat, score edges. Place in a shallow baking dish and bake, uncovered in a 300°F (150°C) oven for 1 hour, until heated through.

Drain cherries, reserving juice. Add enough water to cherry juice to measure 3/4 cup (175 mL) and heat in a small saucepan.

Combine sugar, flour, mustard and salt; add to cherry juice and cook over medium heat, stirring until thickened. Stir in lemon rind, food colouring, if using, and cherries. Heat through. Pour sauce over ham, and bake 30 minutes more.

To serve, cut ham in slices and spoon cherry sauce over them.

Makes 8 servings, with leftovers.

ingredients

3 lb (1.5 kg) centre cut fully cooked
   bone-in ham, about 2 1/2 inches
   (6 cm) thick

1 (14 ounce/398 mL) can sour cherries

1/2 cup (125 mL) sugar

2 tablespoons (30 mL) flour or cornstarch

1/4 teaspoon (1 mL) dry mustard

pinch of salt

2 teaspoons (10 mL) grated lemon rind

2–3 drops red food colouring (optional)

Maritimes Seafood Casserole

There are many variations of this popular East Coast seafood casserole, but this is the one I most often turn to when a festive dish is required. It can be prepared several hours ahead and refrigerated until needed. Allow to stand at room temperature half an hour before putting in oven. Served with rice and a salad, it makes a wonderful meal any time of the year.

Wash scallops thoroughly and remove the little parts where the scallops have been attached to their shells (these have a bitter taste). If scallops are large, cut in half.

Wipe fillets with a damp paper towel; cut into bite-sized pieces. Cut lobster meat into chunks.

In a large saucepan, bring about 2 quarts (2 L) water to a boil; add 1 teaspoon (5 mL) of salt. Add scallops and simmer about 2 minutes. Add haddock and cook 3 minutes, or until fish turns white and flakes easily. Drain. Add lobster to the drained seafood. Refrigerate.

Melt butter in top of a double boiler. Add flour and mustard; cook, stirring for 2 to 3 minutes to remove raw taste of flour. Stir in salt and pepper. Gradually add milk, stirring constantly. Add wine and cook, stirring frequently, until thickened (about 15 minutes). Add Worcestershire and 2 tablespoons (30 mL) parmesan cheese.

Pour sauce over seafood. Add mushrooms. Transfer to a large, lightly-greased casserole dish.

Combine bread crumbs, melted butter and 2 tablespoons (30 mL) grated parmesan cheese; sprinkle on top of casserole. Bake at 350°F (180°C) until

ingredients

1 pound (500 g) scallops

1 pound (500 g) haddock fillets

1 pound (500 g) cooked lobster (thaw, if frozen)

1/2 cup (125 mL) butter

1/2 cup (125 mL) flour

1/2 teaspoon (2 mL) dry mustard

1/2 teaspoon (2 mL) salt

1/4 teaspoon (1 mL) white pepper

4 cups (1 L) milk

1/4 cup (50 mL) white wine or sherry

2 teaspoons (10 mL) Worcestershire sauce

2 tablespoons (30 mL) grated parmesan cheese

2 (10 ounce/284 mL) cans sliced mushrooms, drained

1 cup (250 mL) soft bread crumbs

2 tablespoons (30 mL) butter

2 tablespoons (30 mL) grated parmesan cheese

East Coast Boiled Lobster

Here in Atlantic Canada, many lobster aficionados claim the best way to cook their favourite crustaceans is to boil them in sea water. Some opt for steaming. But most prefer the traditional Down East way of boiling, with a close eye to the timer. Overcooking toughens the meat.

Fill a large pot with enough water to cover the lobsters that will go into the pot (no more than three at a time). Add 1/4 cup (50 mL) salt for each quart (litre) of water. Toss in 1 or 2 extra tablespoons (15–30 mL) "for the pot." Bring water to a vigorous boil.

Pick up a live lobster by the back and plunge it, head first, into the water to ensure death is instantaneous. Do the same with one or two more lobsters. Don't crowd the pot.

Cover pot and cook according to weight of a single lobster: 10 to 12 minutes for 1 to 1 1/2 pounds (500 to 750 g); 15 to 18 minutes for 1 1/2 to 2 pounds (750 g to 1 kg) and 20 to 25 minutes for 2 1/2 to 5 pounds (1 1/4 to 2 1/2 kg).

Plunge cooked lobster immediately into cold water to prevent overcooking them. Drain well before serving with melted butter.

ingredients

Salt

Lobster

Melted butter

Make Your Own Holiday Centrepiece

Dress your table with this festive craft

Story and Photography by Kevin Yarr

Getting Ready

A centrepiece made from natural greenery brings a little light to your table, brightening the holiday feast. Bernadette Praught, of Hearts and Flowers in Charlottetown, offered us these suggestions for a beautiful yet relatively easy-to-make centrepiece.

You may be able to gather most of the materials you'll need from your house and backyard, but they should also be available from any good florist. When making your selection, think about the different textures and shades of green the leaves will give your centrepiece. Green berries can also add texture and colour. Red accents are a must for Christmas.

You could choose gold-painted foliage, white pine and cedar for a very elegant look. For this piece, we chose materials of a more rustic variety. Other common selections could include holly or fresh fruit. There is a wide variety of imported greenery available.

Instructions

Cut as large a piece of floral foam as will comfortably fit into your bowl. This will water your greenery through the life of the centrepiece. Next put in your candles: two is traditional.

Cutting the end of your candles on an angle will allow you to push them more easily into the floral foam.

Now comes the greenery, built from the bottom edge of your floral foam and up towards the top. Start with the greenery you will use the most, providing a frame for everything else going into the piece. The frame should be oblong, to reflect the shape of your table. Cut the ends of your greenery at an angle with a knife, not pruning shears, which will pinch the stems and impede the flow of water. Scrape the

needles from the end of the stem going into the floral foam.

Complete the evergreen frame with red pine, which provides a bold texture. Red pine tends to have strong curves, which you should work with to create the shape of your piece.

Next come the pine cones. These can be wired together in pairs and attached to a green pick. Pairing the cones allows the use of more of them without cluttering. The green pick also assures a firm attachment.

The main accents on this centrepiece are pine cones, salall (broad leaf green), hypericum (red berries), and flat berry eucalyptus (small green berries). These accents are laid down in triangle shapes one at a time, working up toward the top of the floral foam—three pairs of pine cones, three sprigs of salall, three bunches of hypericum, three sprigs of eucalyptus. As you work towards the top of the piece be careful to cover the floral foam, and keep turning the piece to see how it is looking from all sides. Don't be bound by too many restrictions—Bernadette added two bunches of china berries as a final accent, not three. Though the rule of three works well for this size of centrepiece, a theme of five or seven would be more appropriate for a larger one.

And voilà, you have a centrepiece suitable for a table of twelve to fifteen people.

Materials

Evergreens: fir, red pine
Broadleaf greens: Salall, eucalyptus, hypericum
China berries
Pine cones
Flowers
Candles
6-inch shallow bowl
Floral foam
Sharp knife
Florist wire
Green picks

Tip:

You're probably going to have more materials on hand than you need. Avoid the temptation to use them all. The easiest mistake to make is to do too much. "Less is more," says Bernadette. "Crafters tend to overdo it. We have to know when to say when."

vegetables

If there's one vegetable (besides the potato) that dominates the holiday season here in Atlantic Canada, it must truly be the turnip. More recently dubbed rutabaga by the federal department of agriculture (perhaps to raise its image), turnip it remains to the stubborn Down East population that loves it. This hardy root vegetable was grown in early Acadian gardens, and was often roasted whole on the edge of the fire. Some Acadians remember turnips being kept under the beds in unheated upstairs rooms. For some, biting into a raw icy turnip is nostalgic indeed.

Another vegetable grown in those early gardens was cabbage. Farmers would pull them from the earth after the first frost and leave them in the fields to freeze for the winter. It was simply a matter of digging through the snowdrifts to reclaim one. Cabbage has become the stuff of life in these parts.

Topping off the big three is broccoli, a cruciferous vegetable whose popularity has skyrocketed within the last 20 or so years. Almost unknown to a generation past, these "little trees" have displaced peas as the green vegetable on many holiday tables. Its "cousin," cauliflower, always used to be cooked and smothered in cheese. Today it is steamed, boiled, blanched, microwaved, stir-fried, baked, sautéed, souffléd, or for holiday pleasure, cooked in a casserole dotted with chopped red and green peppers.

But the king of all vegetables is, was, and hopefully will be the potato. New Brunswick's and PEI's economies rest largely on this tuber, which is currently going through hard times, in part due to a propensity of low-carb diets. My take on the trend? Abandon the over-processed potato, but keep the real one on your plate! Who can picture a holiday dinner without potatoes? If the low-carb fad persists, Atlantic Canadians are apt to dig their heels in and object…

Mashed Potatoes with Parsnips

Russet Burbanks are an excellent choice for fluffy, dry mashed potatoes. For best results, mash the cooked potatoes by hand or with a hand mixer rather than a food processor, which tends to make them gummy.

Peel and cut potatoes into chunks of about the same size. Peel and slice parsnips. Place potatoes, parsnips, sliced onions and garlic in a large saucepan. Add water to almost cover, bring to a boil. Cover, and boil gently until tender, about 15 to 20 minutes. Drain well.

Mash with a potato masher. Gradually add as much milk as needed for desired consistency, and beat with a fork until light and fluffy. Stir in butter, nutmeg, salt, pepper, and chives, blending well. Makes 8 servings.

ingredients

8 large dry potatoes

1 pound (500 g) parsnips (about 4)

2 medium onions, sliced

3 cloves garlic, peeled, sliced

3/4 to 1 cup (175–250 mL) milk

1/4 cup (50 mL) butter

1/4 teaspoon (1 mL) grated nutmeg

Salt and freshly ground pepper, to taste

3/4 cup (175 mL) chopped chives

Holiday Cauliflower

The green and red peppers in this recipe not only add an extra measure of vitamin C but also give the dish a festive appeal. This dish can be prepared ahead and refrigerated until about an hour before serving time. After it has returned to room temperature, it can be reheated in the microwave, or popped into the oven for half an hour after the turkey is removed.

In a saucepan, bring 1 inch (2.5 cm) of water to a boil. Add the prepared cauliflower and return to the boil. Cook uncovered for 2 to 3 minutes. Reduce heat, cover and cook for 3 to 4 minutes, until cauliflower is just barely cooked. Drain and set aside.

Meanwhile, heat the oil in a large skillet and add the chopped green and red peppers. Sauté for 4 to 5 minutes. Add the drained cauliflower and cook until just tender. Season to taste with salt and pepper. Makes 6 servings.

ingredients

1 medium-sized head of cauliflower, rinsed and broken into florets

2 tablespoons (30 mL) canola oil

1 medium-sized green pepper, chopped coarsely

1 medium-sized red pepper, chopped coarsely

Salt and freshly-ground black pepper

Hot Kohl Slaw

Hot cabbage slaw is a favourite Lunenburg, NS, dish, frequently served with roast turkey. It's better to slice the cabbage thinly using a sharp knife; shredding makes it too fine. For convenience, you can slice the cabbage ahead and store in a sealed plastic bag in the refrigerator.

Combine the vinegar, sugar, tarragon, and salt in a large covered skillet. Bring to a boil over medium heat. Add the prepared cabbage and cook, stirring frequently, for 15 minutes, or until cabbage is just tender. Do not overcook. Remove from heat and stir in the apple. Serve hot. Makes 6 servings.

ingredients

3 tablespoons (45 mL) cider vinegar

1 teaspoon (5 mL) sugar

1/4 teaspoon (1 mL) dried tarragon

1 teaspoon (5 mL) salt

8 cups (2 L) very thinly sliced cabbage

1 large red apple, cut into 1/2 inch (1 cm) cubes

Turnip Loaf

I grew up on turnips, the yellow kind that, along with carrots, kept us going through the winter. When they started calling them rutabagas, I never adapted. To me, it smacked of putting on airs or a marketing ploy, like calling flounder "sole." This dish can be prepared ahead, and reheated for half an hour in a 350°F (180°C) oven before serving.

In a saucepan, cover turnips with boiling water and cook 15 to 20 minutes or until tender. Drain and mash. Season with pepper and nutmeg. Add cream and eggs. Spoon into a greased 9x5-inch (23x13 cm) loaf pan.

Toss bread crumbs with melted butter and sprinkle over turnip. Bake at 375°F (190°C) for 1 hour. Makes 6 to 8 servings.

ingredients

2 small turnips, peeled and diced, (about 6 cups)

1/8 teaspoon (0.5 mL) pepper

1/8 teaspoon (0.5 mL) ground nutmeg

1/2 cup (125 mL) light cream or milk

2 eggs, lightly beaten

1/4 cup (50 mL) soft bread crumbs

1 tablespoon (15 mL) butter, melted

Broccoli with Lemon Crumbs

Broccoli hadn't been "invented" when I stepped into my first kitchen. In fact, I think our sons made it to their teens before they found these little trees on their plates. It was during the '70s that broccoli came into its own. Now available year round, it is probably the most popular green vegetable. To avoid last-minute confusion, have the broccoli cut up and stored in a sealed plastic bag in the refrigerator.

ingredients
Head of broccoli, cut into florets

2 tablespoons (30 mL) butter

2 tablespoons (30 mL) fine bread crumbs

2 teaspoons (10 mL) lemon juice

Make a 1/2-inch (1.3 cm) slit through bottom of each floret to ensure even cooking.

Steam or boil broccoli in as little water as possible, keeping the lid off for the first 5 minutes of cooking to preserve the fresh green colour. Cook 10 minutes or until just tender. Drain.

Melt butter in a small saucepan. Add bread crumbs and sauté for 1 to 2 minutes. Stir in lemon juice. Spoon over broccoli on plates. Makes 4 servings.

Carrots Vichy

Carrots cooked this way are not only dressed for company but they also retain most of their valuable nutrients. To avoid last-minute kitchen confusion, cut the carrots ahead and refrigerate in a sealed plastic bag with a dampened paper towel. Parsley can be chopped and stored separately in the same way.

ingredients
8 medium carrots

2 tablespoons (30 mL) water

1 tablespoon (15 mL) lemon juice

4 tablespoons (60 mL) butter, melted

Dash of nutmeg

Dash of sugar

Dash each of salt and pepper

Chopped parsley

Peel and cut carrots into thin 2-inch (5 cm) strips.

In a saucepan with a tight-fitting cover, combine water, lemon juice, butter, nutmeg, sugar, salt and pepper. Add carrots, cover and cook very gently until tender. Since all liquid will be absorbed, check frequently to prevent scorching.

Toss in a generous amount of chopped parsley. Serve. Makes 4 to 5 servings.

This vegetable dish can be made a day ahead. Cover with foil and store in the refrigerator. Remove from refrigerator at least half an hour before reheating, covered, in a 350°F (180°C) oven, for 30 minutes.

Baked Butternut Squash with Apples and Maple Syrup

Cook squash in boiling water until almost tender, about 3 minutes. Drain. Combine with apples and currants in a 13x9-inch (34x23 cm) glass baking dish.

Season with nutmeg, salt and pepper.

Whisk maple syrup, butter and lemon juice over low heat until butter melts; pour over squash mixture; toss. Bake at 350ºF (180ºC) for about 1 hour, stirring occasionally, until squash and apples are tender and the mixture is heated through. Makes 12 servings.

ingredients

6 cups (1.5 L) peeled, quartered, seeded butternut squash, cut into 1/4-inch (5 mm) slices

6 cups (1.5 L) peeled, quartered, cored tart apples, cut into 1/4-inch (5 mm) slices

3/4 cup (175 mL) dried currants

Ground nutmeg, to taste

Salt and pepper, to taste

3/4 cup (175 mL) pure maple syrup

1/4 cup (50 mL) butter, cut into pieces

1 1/2 tablespoons (22 mL) fresh lemon juice

fixings

If turkey with all the fixings is the order of the day for your Christmas dinner, you already know what the main attraction will be. But what about those fixings? There are decisions to be made.

If you plan to serve the same vegetables that your mother and grandmother chose before you, you may want to add your own twist to them. It may be nothing more than adding a couple of tablespoons of finely chopped ginger or garlic (or both) to your mashed turnip, but it's a way of making your own statement. You can also embellish your mother's plain mashed potatoes in one of several ways. Try adding feta or blue cheese, sour cream or yogurt, ricotta or cream cheese, parmesan or cheddar cheese, fresh dill or chive blossoms, roasted garlic or onions. Or, mash the potatoes with another vegetable, such as turnip, celery root, sweet potatoes, or parsnips. You can simply enrich them with heavy cream, or lighten them with buttermilk. What's important here is that there are mashed potatoes for your holiday dinner.

Cranberries, in one form or another, are also traditional holiday fare. It can be as simple as boiling the cranberries is a sugar syrup until they pop, or as wonderfully delicious as the Baked Cranberry Walnut Relish included here.

If mincemeat pie is on the menu, you will want to have your mincemeat made in advance of the pie-making. Try our recipe for green tomato mincemeat. It's really good. You may even want to make enough to give as gifts, or go a step further and make the pies for those friends who don't make their own.

If you're as smart as I think you are, you'll be doing as much advance preparation as possible. Vegetable dishes can be prepared ahead and stored in the freezer or refrigerator to be thawed and reheated before serving. Desserts, also, are ready and waiting.

Comes the time for serving and all is in order. Except the gravy. Ah! There's the snag. So, let us wish you a merry Christmas by giving you directions for Make-ahead Gravy.

Make-ahead Gravy

Turkey dinners often go smoothly until it's time to make the gravy. Then, the juggling begins. The turkey comes out of the oven to "rest" on a platter; the make-ahead vegetables go in to reheat; and the plates are warming. It's then that the gravy making begins. Unless you have a huge kitchen with a lot of counter space, and a magician's knack at having everything hot and ready at the same time, you could stand a little help. That isn't so easy to get in a small kitchen.

So, here's some advance help: make the gravy up to a month ahead and save the turmoil, frustration and possible accidents.

Place turkey pieces in roasting pan; lightly brush with oil. Roast at 350°F (180°C) for 2 hours or until turkey pieces are a deep golden brown. Transfer turkey to a large pot. Add vegetables to a large pot. To the roasting pan, add 2 cups (500 mL) water; bring to a boil over medium heat, stirring to loosen brown bits. Add to pot with turkey. Add 2 quarts (2 L) water to pot and bring to a boil. Reduce heat and simmer, partially covered, for 1 1/2 hours. Remove turkey parts; reserve for another use.

Strain liquid through a sieve; pour into containers and store in refrigerator overnight. Skim and discard fat from top of stock. (Can be prepared to this point and stored in refrigerator for up to 24 hours or in freezer for up to a month. Thaw in refrigerator before using.)

To make gravy, measure liquid and reheat gently. For each cup of stock, use 1 tablespoon (15 mL) butter and 1 tablespoon (15 mL) all-purpose flour.

Melt butter in a Dutch oven over low heat. Stir in flour and cook for 2 minutes. Don't let flour brown. Remove from heat and add stock, whisking continuously. Return to heat and cook, whisking constantly, until gravy is smooth and thickened. Season to taste with salt and pepper. Remove from heat, partially cool and pour into freezer containers in required amounts. Makes about 10 cups gravy.

To reheat, transfer from freezer to refrigerator a couple of days before serving. Bring to a simmer and serve.

ingredients

2 turkey legs

2 turkey wings

Canola oil

3 carrots, cut into chunks

3 ribs celery, cut into chunks

1 medium onion, quartered

2 tablespoons (30 mL) chopped fresh parsley

4 teaspoons (20 mL) chicken bouillon powder

1/2 teaspoon (2 mL) thyme, crumbled

1/2 teaspoon (2 mL) salt

1/2 teaspoon (2 mL) pepper

Green Tomato Mincemeat

If you have a vegetable garden and green tomatoes that don't look like they're going to ripen before the frost, you can get an early start on your holiday baking. Make up a batch of green tomato mincemeat. When it's time to make the pies, no one will ever know it isn't the real thing. And look at the all the money you've saved!

In a large stainless steel or enamel pot or Dutch oven, combine tomatoes, apples, raisins, peels, spices, salt, sugars, apple juice, vinegar, and lemon juice. Bring to a boil over medium-high heat. Reduce heat to medium-low and gently cook for 1 1/2 hours, stirring frequently. Remove from heat and stir in rum or brandy.

Ladle into hot sterilized mason jars and process in a hot water bath for 15 minutes. Makes 5 to 6 pint (500 mL) jars.

To make mincemeat pie, see page 14.

ingredients

- 8 cups (2 L) chopped cored green tomatoes (unpeeled)
- 4 cups (1 L) chopped peeled apples
- 3 cups (750 mL) raisins
- 1/2 cup (125 mL) mixed candied peel
- 1/4 cup (50 mL) candied orange peel
- 2 teaspoons (10 mL) ground cinnamon
- 1 teaspoon (5 mL) ground ginger
- 1/2 teaspoon (2 mL) ground cloves
- 1/2 teaspoon (2 mL) ground allspice
- 1/2 teaspoon (2 mL) grated nutmeg
- 1 teaspoon (5 mL) salt
- 1 1/2 cups (375 mL) granulated sugar
- 1 cup (250 mL) lightly packed brown sugar
- 1 cup (250 mL) apple juice
- 1/3 cup (75 mL) cider vinegar
- 2 tablespoons (30 mL) lemon juice
- 1/2 cup (125 mL) rum or brandy

Baked Cranberry Relish

Toasted walnuts add a wonderful crunch and flavour to this oven-baked cranberry relish. To toast the walnuts, spread in a single layer on a rimmed baking sheet and place in a preheated 35°F (180°C) oven for 12 to 15 minutes.

Apart from serving with poultry or ham, try spooning the relish over waffles, pancakes, or warm over ice cream. Delicious!

Spread cranberries in a 13x9-inch (34x23 cm) baking dish; sprinkle evenly with sugar and water. Cover tightly with foil. Bake at 325°F (160°C) for 30 to 45 minutes or until cranberries start to pop, shaking pan once or twice during baking.

Remove from oven, stir in marmalade, citrus juice, and nuts. Spoon into a bowl or jars, cover, and chill for at least 3 hours before serving.

Makes 3 1/2 cups (875 mL).

ingredients

- 4 cups (1 L) fresh cranberries, washed, dried
- 1 1/2 cups (375 mL) granulated sugar
- 2 tablespoons (30 mL) water
- 1 cup (250 mL) orange marmalade
- Juice of 1 lime or lemon
- 1 cup (250 mL) coarsely chopped walnuts, toasted

turkey leftovers

Those who, with their families, moan and groan after too many reappearances of leftover turkey, probably don't use much imagination when planning those meals. It doesn't take much effort to change those groans to cheers. Rule number one is "Never make the same dish from the same turkey." Variety does more for leftovers than even a generous helping of gravy can.

The second-day application is often turkey sandwiches, a tradition that no one seems to want to break. Imagination takes over after that. For instance, there's turkey hash patties, made by grinding some of the cooked turkey and mixing with a raw egg, chopped onions, herbs, salt and pepper, and shaping the mixture into patties before sautéing them in a little oil.

It's fun, too, to fondue. An easy sauce can be prepared with a can of condensed cream soup of your choice, 1/4 cup (50 mL) milk and 1 cup (250 mL) of shredded cheese, into which cubes of cooked turkey can be dipped.

If there is still enough turkey to cut into cubes, toss them into a fruit salad, made with apple, pear, and/or chunks of canned peaches, toasted slivered almonds, shredded lettuce and creamy dressing.

Still more? Chop and stir into a package of macaroni-and-cheese dinner along with 1/2 teaspoon (2 ml) of tarragon and a little sour cream or plain yogurt.

Next year, you might align yourself with the majority. These are the people who buy a much larger turkey than needed for the holiday dinner. They do it in order to display their creativity in bringing several different economical meals to the table. Kudos to them—and to you.

Warm Turkey Salad

With a large turkey providing about 40 per cent of its purchased weight in edible meat, smart cooks will delight in having the protein base for additional meals. Others may wonder what to do with it all. The recipes in this section offer choices that are sure to be welcomed by both groups.

To prepare vinaigrette: Mix all ingredients except ginger. Peel ginger, cut into small dice and add to vinaigrette.

To prepare salad: Cut cooked turkey into strips; set aside. Wash romaine lettuce and dry well, then break into pieces and set on cold plates. Cut peppers into coarse julienne strips. Cut onion into 1/4 inch (5 mm) slices.

In a large pan, saute all ingredients, starting with the onion, then mushrooms, peppers, and finally the turkey. Cook until vegetables are tender. Pour 1 cup (250 mL) of the vinaigrette over the vegetables and turkey. Arrange mixture over romaine lettuce and garnish with chopped nuts and parsley. Makes 4 servings.

ingredients

vinaigrette

1 cup (250 mL) vinegar

1 cup (250 mL) soy sauce (unsalted, if possible)

1/2 cup (125 mL) lightly packed brown sugar

5 cloves garlic, chopped

1 1/2 inch (4 cm) piece of fresh gingerroot

salad

3 cups (750 g) cooked turkey breast or leg

1 head romaine lettuce

1 yellow pepper

1 red pepper

1 green pepper

1 red onion

20 mushrooms

garnishes

Chopped walnuts (about 1/2 cup/125 mL) and chopped parsley

Turkey Brunch Casserole

When everyone else is tidying up and putting their gifts away, you could be in the kitchen preparing the next day's brunch. Although this dish can be ready for the oven after only an hour's standing, it is better when it sits in the refrigerator overnight so the bread can absorb the custard more effectively.

Line a buttered 13x9-inch (33x23 cm) baking dish with 6 of the bread slices. Brush with melted butter. Layer with half of each of the turkey, grated cheese and green onions. Top with remaining bread slices and brush with butter. Add remaining turkey, cheese and green onions.

Beat eggs with milk and seasonings; pour over bread. Let rest for half an hour at room temperature, then cover and refrigerate overnight, or for several hours.

Bake at 375°F (190°C) for 45 to 50 minutes or until crisp, puffed and golden. Cut into 6 portions and serve with cranberry sauce or maple syrup. Makes 6 servings.

ingredients

12 slices bread

1/4 cup (50 mL) melted butter

8 ounces (250 g) thinly sliced cooked turkey

8 ounces (250 g) grated cheddar cheese

4–6 green onions, finely chopped

8 eggs

3 cups (750 mL) milk

1/2 teaspoon (2 mL) dried summer savoury

Salt and pepper to taste

Turkey Pita Pockets

A word or two about food safety: Once the turkey is carved, and extra placed on a platter for second helpings, the rest of the turkey and stuffing should be kept in a 250°F (120°C) oven. Turkey, or other poultry, should not stand at room temperature longer than two hours. When storing, remove turkey from the bone and refrigerate in shallow containers so it cools quickly; use within 4 days. Stuffing and gravy should be stored separately and used within 2 days.

In a bowl, combine turkey, apples, carrot, celery, nuts, tarragon, mayonnaise and Italian dressing. Mix well. Refrigerate for 1 hour to blend flavours. Stir in salad greens.

Cut pita breads in half to form pockets. Stuff each pocket with turkey mixture and top with sprouts. Makes 8 servings.

ingredients

3 cups (750 mL) cooked, cubed turkey

2 apples, unpeeled, chopped

1 carrot, grated

2 ribs celery, cut in small dice

1/2 cup (125 mL) walnuts or pecans, chopped

1 teaspoon (5 mL) fresh chopped tarragon, optional

1 cup (250 mL) mayonnaise

1/4 cup (50 mL) Italian dressing

2 cups (500 mL) chopped salad greens (lettuce or spinach)

8 individual pita breads

Alfalfa sprouts

The Sweet Taste of Tradition

Certain things in life just can't be improved upon

The holidays were approaching when a woman and her daughter overheard a group of college students talking in a Toronto snack bar. Excitement built among the group as, one by one, they spoke of their plans to go home for Christmas. When one remained silent, his peers pressed him for an answer.

"No, my parents have given everything they can to help pay for my tuition, and I just can't afford to go home to the Maritimes for Christmas," he said. "What I'm going to miss most is the ribbon candy we always get at Christmas."

Was it a Christmas miracle that guided that woman to that particular snack bar to overhear that conversation? Maybe, for she was the wife of the national accounts manager for Robertson's Candy, of Truro, Nova Scotia, the very firm that had been producing ribbon candy for close to 75 years. And was it fate that caused the woman to take her husband's car that night, (something she never does) in the trunk of which was one full box of ribbon candy? The woman went to the car, and on returning, approached the group.

"I couldn't help overhearing your conversation," she said, singling out the Maritimer. "I want you to have this box of ribbon candy."

This is when the tears may flow, as they did for the young man, who actually got down on his knees to thank the woman for

giving him a piece of Christmas tradition that would otherwise have been missing.

Creating even more holiday nostalgia than ribbon candy are the moulded red and yellow clear toys, often called barley toys (or shapes, or animals).

"Clear toys are a family tradition in the Maritimes," says the company owner Roy Robertson, popularly known as the Candy Man. He often hears nostalgic stories about his candy from transplanted Atlantic Canadians, who send orders from as far away as New Zealand, Saudi Arabia, and Bosnia.

The candy is made today exactly as it was 75 years ago. Most of the original equipment is still in use, and Roy's collection of Thomas Mills moulds, numbered in the thousands, is thought to be the largest in the world.

Apart from flavouring and colouring, only three ingredients are used in the making of Christmas candies—sugar, corn syrup and water. After boiling to the proper temperature in a large open copper pot, the mixture is dipped out by long-handled ladles and rushed to the cold room where chilled moulds are set up waiting to

receive it. Sucker sticks are put in place as it cools, and when the mixture has cooled enough, the two-piece moulds are opened, the edges trimmed if necessary, and the finished product goes on trays to be packed into 284-gram bags and sealed.

It's labour-intensive work because everything, from the weighing of ingredients to the packaging, is done by hand. Even the pulling to incorporate air into what will become the satin-mix hard candies, is hand-done: A large piece of the cooling mixture is spun into a rope, and hung on a large hook on the wall to be pulled and pulled some more, until the mixture turns opaque and is cool enough to handle. Colour is then applied before it goes into a roller machine to be cut into shapes, some long, some flat and some oval.

Here at home all of this sweet stuff is taken for granted. But last year for the first time, clear toys were carried in Zeller's stores across the country. It was a Christmas gift from "the sweetest people in Truro, NS."

Other Atlantic Candy Makers

In St. Stephen, NB, Ganong's turns out the popular chicken bones (invented in 1885). Described as chocolate turned inside out, with a generous strand of unsweetened chocolate under a jacket of pink spicy cinnamon candy, chicken bones are another Maritime tradition that provokes a lot of sentiment, especially at holiday time.

Purity Factories Limited in St. John's, NL, produce a sought-after treat in the province and beyond: peppermint nobs (knobs). These pink, hand-sugared candies have been made since the 1920s, not only for Christmas, but all year round.

A Sweet Ending

Marie's claim to culinary fame: Fudge!

Fudge making is not the awesome task some people think it is, but, as with most worthwhile endeavours, there are rules to be followed. Rule number one for me is to never make fudge on a rainy day. High humidity plays havoc with sugar crystals and the fudge may turn out lumpy, or at best, sugary. Since I like my fudge to be creamy, I wait for a clear day.

I find it best to use a heavy, flat-bottomed saucepan with high sides to prevent spillovers. Butter the sides of the pot so that grains of sugar cannot cling and start crystallizing. If crystals do form, brush them down with a pastry brush that has been dipped in hot water.

Watch the boiling process carefully, testing frequently toward the end of the cooking time to determine if the soft ball stage has been reached. I always double check this by using both a candy thermometer and the old-fashioned cold water method, which is as follows:

Have some ice cold water in a cup. Remove saucepan from heat so it doesn't continue to cook and drop about 1/2 teaspoon (2 mL) of the hot mixture into the water. Let stand 1 minute. Then pick the mixture up between your thumb and index finger: if it makes a soft ball, but doesn't hold its shape, it has reached the soft ball stage. If it fails to do that, return to the heat for another couple of minutes. Test again, and again if necessary, until it's ready to be turned into fudge.

If I have one claim to culinary fame, it has to be my fudge. Every year, as Christmas approached, I devoted many a fine day to making up several batches, not only for my family but to give as gifts, as well. As long as I had help with the beating, I would turn out one batch after the other. Finally, in November of 1991, it caught up with me. Seven continuous hours of fudge making brought on a stress fracture in my left foot. When, in great pain, I went to see a doctor and told him the story of what had happened, he gained much pleasure in telling his colleagues about the patient who "fudged up her foot." Still, there was fudge for Christmas.

ingredients

- 4 cups (1 L) packed brown sugar
- 1 cup (250 mL) evaporated milk
- 1/4 cup (50 mL) butter or margarine (in 1 piece)
- 1 teaspoon (5 mL) vanilla
- 3/4 cup (175 mL) chopped nuts or desiccated coconut

In a large, heavy-bottomed saucepan, combine sugar, milk and butter. Stir over moderate heat until butter had melted and sugar has dissolved. Bring to a boil. Clip candy thermometer in place, making sure it is deep into the mixture but does not touch the bottom of the pan. Cook, stirring, until mixture reaches the soft ball stage (238°F/115°C).

Remove from heat and, leaving thermometer in place, set the pot in the sink with enough cold water to come halfway up the side of the pot. Cool to 110°F (44°C). Don't move the saucepan while cooling or sugar crystals may start to form.

Stir in vanilla. Beat vigorously until fudge begins to lose its gloss and seems to stiffen. Add chopped nuts or coconut. Work quickly to push mixture from saucepan into a buttered 8 or 9 inch (20 or 23 cm) square pan with rubber spatula or wooden spurtle. Don't scrape sides.

Score fudge while still warm and cut when cold. Makes 25 or 36 pieces, depending on size of pan.

Variation: To make chocolate fudge, mix 3 tablespoons (45 mL) cocoa powder with the sugar.

recipe index